MATTHEW ARNOLD'S PROSE

AMS STUDIES IN THE NINETEENTH CENTURY, NO. 3

Other titles in this series:

1. Anne Aresty Naman. *The Jew in the Victorian Novel.* 1980.
2. Sue Lonoff. *Wilkie Collins and His Victorian Readers.* 1982.

ISSN: 0196-657X

MATTHEW ARNOLD'S PROSE

Three Essays in Literary Enlargement

William E. Buckler

AMS PRESS, INC.
New York

Library of Congress Cataloging in Publication Data

Buckler, William Earl, 1924-
Matthew Arnold's prose.

(AMS studies in the nineteenth century, ISSN 0196-657X ; no. 3)

Includes bibliographical references and index.
Contents: Literature and dogma and literature—The poetics of Matthew Arnold's prose—Facing the enemy within.
1. Arnold, Matthew, 1822-1888—Prose works—Addresses, essays, lectures. I. Title. II. Series.
PR4024.B77 1983 828'.809 83-45276
ISBN 0-404-61481-7

MANUFACTURED IN THE UNITED STATES OF AMERICA

For Borg

Acknowledgments

A version of Chapter I appeared in *The Victorian Newsletter* (Spring, 1981). I am grateful to the editor for permission to reprint.

The text of Arnold used is that of *The Complete Prose Works of Matthew Arnold,* ed. R. H. Super (Ann Arbor: University of Michigan Press, 1960–1977). Like all Arnold scholars, I am deeply indebted to the editor and the publishers for this superb edition.

Contents

Introduction

The bold assertion by Matthew Arnold's latest and only genuine biographer that "an understanding of [Arnold] is really more useful to us than an understanding of any other Englishman of the last century,"[1] though clearly hyperbolic, is a sign of the times. Arnold's critical stock is rising again as new generations of literary students "endeavour to learn and practise, amid the bewildering confusion of our times, what is sound and true"[2] in the way of criticism. It will be a somewhat turbulent rise, not because of the volatility of various contemporary schools of criticism, but because of the re-emergence, in the wake of a general dissatisfaction with the partiality and aggressiveness of their activities, of some of the fundamental questions affecting our sense of the character of literature and of its intellectual, cultural, and aesthetic worth.

Arnold has much to contribute to the renewed dialogue on these basic literary questions, especially for those whose primary interest is in literature itself rather than in the contentions among critical systems. Like Dryden, Johnson, and Coleridge before him, and like Pater afterwards, Arnold brought a new imaginative idiom, wonderfully rich, comprehensive, and proportionate, to the study of Western literature. He still speaks with the freshness inherent in unique imaginative insight and the authority that comes of attention to the fundamental issues implicit in one's subject, despite periodic shifts in critical fashions.

Arnold came to criticism from poetry, and he brought the poet's vision with him. To the critic's desire to enlighten, Arnold added the poet's desire to transform, and "enlightened transformation" is a fair designation of the motive that fueled Arnold's prose—of the new quality that he implanted in English criticism and passed on to Pater. It has had a somewhat random history since Arnold implanted it in the third quarter of the nineteenth century, and Pater subjected it to a dramatic transformation of temperament in the fourth quarter, but it has been one of the chief sustainers of our century's wayward humanism.

It is, indeed, the humanist point at which Plato and Aristotle, Hellenism and Hebraism, Saint Augustine and Bishop Wilson, Sophocles and Dante, Marcus Aurelius and Newman, Newton and Goethe and Wordsworth and Hegel and Heinrich Heine, and all the other struggling, fallible, and exemplary human beings who populate Arnold's pages, touch and reciprocate each other and radiate outward their crucial significance. It is the point at which aesthetics, ethics, and epistemology—art, action, and scientific philosophy—meet and reinforce each other and mirror the internal condition of man that craves fulfilment at a level both simple and grand. It is what gives dynamic significance to Arnold's principle of "seeing things as they in fact are" and functional value to his "openness of mind" and "flexibility of intelligence": *these premises actually work*, as anyone can demonstrate by simply trying them. When one sees them working, it alters his life—its aspect, its motive, its possibilities. Plato had said it more than two millennia before: "The best man is he who tries to perfect himself, and the happiest man is he who most feels that he *is* perfecting himself"[3]; and through a magnificent act of co-creation with Plato, Arnold made it the source of his moral and imaginative energy and, reinforced with a programme of self-education—of "reading, observing, thinking," the central insight in a literary canon that touches profoundly both our human weariness and our human desire.

Enlightenment alone is not enough: like Hellenism, it is not half enough. The process of transformation is what converts knowledge into relevance and gives it its human magnetism; personal metamorphosis is at once the catalyst and the goal. Human nature, Arnold believed, had an innate need to know; but it also had a similar need to act and, according to its best light, to act well. He shaped his literary canon around this conception of human nature in an all-enveloping aesthetic sense: he chose his subjects, constructed his architecture, and monitored his language so as to induce both the perception and the process.

The essays in this volume seek to enlarge the reader's understanding of Matthew Arnold's essential literariness, to show how basically dependent his critical affectiveness is upon his literary art. In one sense, they imply that Arnold was much more than a great critic—that he was a great literary moralist in the tradition of Aesop and Swift and a great literary humanist in the tradition of Plato. But while that is true and needs to be said, it is also true that one cannot be a great critic in a truly holistic sense without being a great moralist and a great humanist since that is, after all, the function of the critic because that is the function of literature. "Total" critics are, of course, very rare, as illustrated by the fact that Arnold is without peer even in the nineteenth century, our first grand epoch of creative criticism in English. However, we do know from his example what a total critic is, and it seems eminently salutary to look at Arnold as closely as possible both to see him as he really is and to enlarge our "whole view and rule" of criticism, according to our individual sympathy and capacity. The purpose of such a close acquaintance with Arnold is not to counter the negligent or hostile attitudes toward him that have been customary in some circles during the last two decades. Such attitudes reflect a presumptive Arnold or a remembered Arnold and tend to take care of themselves. The purpose is the same as that of a generation now reading Tennyson and Hardy with new eyes and pioneering relish: to discover for ourselves how a writer with extraordinary creative gifts implanted in his critical consciousness a profound apprehension of the incomparable character and value of literature and employed the strategies of his literary art to involve his readers in the very process of recognizing that, properly understood, literature can give perspective and value to every dimension of their lives.

NOTES

1. Park Honan, *Matthew Arnold: A Life* (New York: McGraw-Hill Book Company, 1981), p. vii.
2. Arnold's Preface to *Poems* (1853), in *The Complete Prose Works of Matthew Arnold,* ed. R. H. Super (Ann Arbor: University of Michigan Press, 1960), I, 14.
3. Quoted by Arnold in *Culture and Anarchy*. See *Complete Prose Works*, ed. Super, V, 167–168.

Literature and Dogma and Literature

New Textual Perspective on Arnold's Critical Organicism

In a recent essay on the imaginative distinctiveness of Victorian literature, I made the following substantial claim for Matthew Arnold as a literary critic:

> What Matthew Arnold did for literary criticism . . . was to bring the critical act so close to the creative act that criticism's generative analogue is clearly visible in the creative work itself, while at the same time he preserved impeccably the discrete distinction between the work of the critic and the work of the creator. He brought the suffusive empiricism of the modern *Zeitgeist*, with its reenforcing counterpart in Aristotelian Classicism, to the service of literary experience. And he did this in two ways: by drawing the intuitions and practical rules of his criticism only from literary experience itself, from a wide, deep, oft-repeated, wholly experimental proofing of the world's great literary texts; and by communicating to his readers the proven, verifiable "*ground* and *authority*" of literature's . . . call on them. Thus Arnold's very mission as a critic was rooted in an irrefragable faith in the organic, transformational, conversional affectiveness of literature which was itself rooted in just such experience. His temperament, the character of his education, his sense of mission, the peculiarities of his life-history, and the *Zeitgeist* had removed Arnold from the confessional mode by which Wordsworth, Coleridge, Carlyle, and Newman gave literary exposure to this sort of conversional experience; but the fact that he used an Aristotelian rather than an Augustinian or a Rousseauistic mode of discourse does not disguise the fact that his personal transformation through literary experience undergirds the character and intensity of his devotion to letters and brings it close to the sort of revelation in which literary experience is itself centered.[1]

Such a manifest faith in the solidity and salutariness of Arnold as a critic of literature, not customary in the curiously fast-stepping, one-sided debate in progress at the present time, demands fuller elaboration than the circumstances surrounding the original assertion allowed. That is the purpose of the present essay. The large proportions of the underlying issue will be perceived by those who recognize that the Deconstructionists have launched not just a corrective to some of our casual ways of dealing with literary texts, but a fundamental attack on the classicism which, with many variations, held steady in the Western critical consciousness from Aristotle to, say, Matthew Arnold. In America, Arnold has become their whipping-boy because, more than anyone else, he re-modernized classicism and made it a pervasive presence in the academic critical mind.

Literature and Dogma: An Essay Towards a Better Apprehension of the Bible (1873) has been chosen as the critical document for demonstration of these and other substantial claims for Arnold's stature and continuing relevance as a literary critic.[2] It is a book somewhat off the beaten path for non-Arnoldians and thus may invite a response minimally cluttered by entrenched prejudices on both the positive and the negative sides. As Arnold's most extensive and detailed study of one of the world's great books—the Bible—it was written at the end of his second decade as a practicing critic, when his critical techniques were at the top of their form and his critical frame of reference and *aperçus* fully developed. While one may consider another of Arnold's books as more original and authoritative (e.g., *On Translating Homer*) or more of a critical landmark (e.g., *Essays in Criticism, First Series*) or bolder (e.g., *On the Study of Celtic Literature*) or more crucial to the century (e.g., *Culture and Anarchy*), everyone will surely admit that *Literature and Dogma* is vintage Arnold and a fair test of his critical method and its significance.

At the heart of *Literature and Dogma* is the issue of epistemological relevance—what and how we can know about matters central to the Bible and how we can translate the verifiable truth of the Bible into our own lives. Both aspects of this issue contribute to the central motive of *Literature and Dogma* and to Arnold's whole career as a critic: that the matter is true (experimentally knowable, verifiable) and that it is "instractable" (fundamentally operative in ourselves if we can master the simple secret of internalization).

For this double renewal—the renewal in our critical understanding of the original meaning of the Bible and the affective beginnings of the moral renewal[3] of ourselves—the crucial key is language. Therefore, *Literature and Dogma* is essentially a critical redemption of language, an erasure of clichés. It is a re-creation of signs, a release of language from the prison of metaphysics, a return of *literary* words to their original and authentic generation in quintessential but fully representative human experience. It is, as well, a rhythmic demonstration that the renewal of language is an archetypal endeavor of men of good sense because language, so indispensable to man's access to fresh knowledge, inevitably degenerates into conventional triteness with the loss of the initial intuition that released it and seems to be the very thing it was originally created to replace.

Arnold says repeatedly that a large part of criticism depends on our understanding of how men use words and what they mean by them. Through the example of Israel (i.e., the Old Testament), he emphasizes how "the spirit and tongue of Israel kept a propriety, a reserve, a sense of the inadequacy of language in conveying man's ideas of God" as contrasted with "the astounding particularity and licence of affirmation" conspicuous in the modern "science" of theology (187, 200) and in the demands for linguistic clarity and definiteness in modern science generally. Poets are the creators and tenders of language, but they, like Israel, are perpetually and painfully aware that language is inadequate to the expression of any truly challenging insight. The poet's words must, therefore, be "*thrown out* at a vast object of consciousness, which he [can] not fully grasp . . ." (187–88). This is not linguistic license or linguistic carelessness, but a sort of linguistic heroism, a determination not to abandon an insight just because language is inadequate to its full expression and a determination not to shrink an insight to the reaches of a perfectly comprehensive language. Unlike the theologian and the scientist who, because they deal in the illusion of the knowable, must make their language and their insights coequal, the poet intuits beyond the easy reach of language, though he constantly attempts to extend language to encompass his furthest-reaching intuitions.

The critic of literature who would become theological or scientific, therefore, can do so only by shrinking literature and, thereby, collapsing his intellectual trust. By transforming ideas so intensely and profoundly intuited that they outstrip the very capacity of langauge, even in the hands of a master of language, into a language that aspires not simply to practical clarity, but to definiteness and comprehensiveness of meaning, the critic falls into the very philosophical or scientific trap from which only literature itself can keep him free or free him after his fall. He becomes a petty or grand systematizer of the ideas and techniques of a language-rooted experience whose authentic significance depends on a rebellion against the inadequacy of systems, including the inadequacy of language-systems. It was in the interests of this supreme literary truth that Arnold avoided a criticism of definitions and employed a critical language that has seemed to some to be too vague to be impressive.

The opposite is in fact true. It is not the vagueness of language that makes Arnold so frustrating to our rage for definiteness. At the practical level, his meaning is eminently clear, and it is so interwoven with apt illustrations of that meaning that, though the idea may be rejected, it can hardly be conscientiously misunderstood. What frustrates many of his readers is his resistance to closure, his refusal to *package* literature, in however brilliant and complexly impressive a fashion. He saw literature as the chief curative to modern man's spiritual malaise, and we have no serious doubt that he saw it that way. But he steadfastly refused to make a talisman or dilettante's toy out of literature, even for the literary professional. He resisted all the pressures of a theologically, philosophically, scientifically positivistic age to make literature's curative way "simpler than possible" (Einstein). He knew that literature, if it were to work authentically, must work organically, that it depended on the very broadest, deepest, most repetitive experience. That was literature's only practical application to the spiritual ills of modern life, and his criticism was most practical when it held truest to that insight. It is an irony of the very keenest sort that, as the modern mentality becomes more positivistic, it hungers more frantically for the myth of the magic wand; as it becomes more habituated to the services of the mechanical self for instant safety and instant gratification, it yearns more for instant growth. And that it cannot have. It may substitute the personal miracle or instant conversion for organic growth, or it may fixate on the idea of quick redemption as a welcome escape from both acute yearning and the necessarily prolonged pain of personal growth.

For the great generality of persons, however, there is no substitute for gradualness, as both Arnold and Tennyson knew: we are, at our best, Arthurians, not Grailites. All great writers have known this, and it is imperative that critics know it too. It is a mark of Arnold's abiding greatness as a critic that he had the courage to resist critical glamour, using critical language as an oblique and parabolic way of insinuating it, organically, into our consciousness. "The language of science about it," says Arnold, "would be *below* what we feel to be the truth" (189) of great literary experience, and a scientific criticism would be below it too.

The severity of Arnold's attendance upon the true meaning of a work's original language, coupled with his extreme care to avoid slipping into a critical language that was reductive of the work's original intuition, is one of the ways in which he brought the critical act close to the creative act. Another is his parabolic or analogical method.

Literature and Dogma is parabolic or analogical in that it talks about one subject in terms that have valid reference to another subject, and this parabolic or analogical method works beautifully for Arnold because both subjects interpenetrate and illumine each other. The central (inner) subject of *Literature and Dogma* is the Bible; the encompassing (outer) subject is the nature of literary experience; the mechanism of the book (its instrument of discovery) is a highly organic form of literary criticism that touches both the inner and outer subjects simultaneously and enables them to unfold together. That this is the implicit and continuous method of his book, Arnold several times signals. For example, he allows one of the central parables underlying *Literature and Dogma*—that revelation takes place only in the consciousness and may come from the literature of Homer, Sophocles, and Shakespeare as well as from the literature of Isaiah—to break through the parabolic texture at the end of the first chapter, "Religion Given," in order to consolidate the fundamental argument of the book.

The distinction between "natural religion" and "revealed religion" is a false distinction: that religion which is most natural is most revealed. "The real antithesis, to natural and revealed alike, is *invented, artificial*" (195); and "*invented, artificial*" religion is the religion, not of the Bible or of any other testament of authentic literary experience, but of theologians. The revelations of consciousness are lost to man to the degree that any scientific theologian or scientific critic erects an artificial religion or an artificial criticism between him and the natural instrument of those revelations, literature:

> For the thing turns upon understanding the manner in which men have thought, their way of using words, and what they mean by them. And by knowing letters, by becoming conversant with the best that has been thought and said in the world, we become acquainted not only with the history, but also with the scope and powers, of the instruments which men employ in thinking and speaking. *And that is just what is sought for* (196, emphasis added).

At the end of Chapter II—"*Aberglaube Invading*"—Arnold again explicitly signals that the inner Biblical literary history (the mutating textual history) that he has been tracing from the initial intuition of the golden age of Hebrew classicism (c. 1000 B. C.) to the hardened Messianic ideas of the second century B. C. has an analogue in the present time: "similar ideas have so signally done the same thing with popular Christianity" (213). This verifies our recognition that throughout the chapter there are unspoken, implicit parallels between the ancient decay of this original intuition and the modern decay of it, including the perennial human inclination to confront the "unworthiness and infelicities of the actual present" with inflated and artificial and hardened anticipations of the future (210).

Thus the *Aberglaube* of antiquity has its parabolic counterpart in the *Aberglaube* of modernism, and the movement toward it follows an archetypal pattern. Further, though Arnold agrees with Goethe that " '*Aberglaube* is the poetry of life,—*der Aberglaube ist die Poesie des Lebens*' " (212), it is not the greatest poetry. Implicit in his tracing of the inner movement from the original intuition to these "more prodigal and wild imaginations" is the contrast between the simplicity, force, and austerity of Hebrew classicism, based on "firm, experimental ground," and this latter-day Romanticism, with its extravagant hope and augury, which has so hardened the original poetic inspiration that it even "imagine[s] itself science." This too has its parabolic analogue in the efforts of Arnold's own century and ours to invent a "science" of the beautiful.

One of Arnold's deftest uses of this parabolic or analogical method can be seen in his treatment and transmutation of the concept of happiness (191–95) as the object of life, as fulfilling the law of our being. Bentham and his followers had implanted happiness as the great object of life in the nineteenth century: pleasure as the test of moral good, the "Greatest Happiness of the Greatest Number" as the test of social good (good government). Happiness had become the cultural measure of the good life, and selfishness (enlightened self-interest) had become its means. A power "*not ourselves,*" a *Zeitgeist* pressure, had made it so, and that pressure was a moral one centered in conduct, both private and public.

Building on this thoroughly verifiable moral disposition of his century but without direct reference to the moral calculus of the Utilitarians, Arnold incrementally undercuts the selfish, epicurean theory of happiness by showing that a power "*not ourselves*" may, unless it is the "*Eternal,*" lead us to disobey "the real law of our being" and leave us unfulfilled. Drawing on a variety of witnesses—St. Paul, Epictetus, Quintillian, Goethe, Bishop Butler, Bishop Wilson, the *Imitation*, Isaac Barrow, Saint Augustine, Proverbs, Psalms, Job, Isaiah—he shows that the testimony overwhelmingly supports virtue and the blessedness and gratitude which virtue induces as the chief law of our permanent self that seeks fulfilment, not the pleasurable gratification sought by the temporary, mechanical, instantaneous, apparent self of a cultural moment or era like the present time. He carries this anti-Utilitarianism even further by contrasting the anti-religious character of the modern morality of "*self-love*" with the jubilee of selflessness celebrated in the Psalms and in Isaiah with such "power and depth of emotion" that *morality* passed into *religion* as "The obligation of a grateful and devout self-surrender to the Eternal replaced all sense of obligation [even] to one's own better self, one's own permanent interest" (194).

But *Literature and Dogma* may be said to vibrate with parabolic analogies. Implicit in the redemption of the Bible is the redemption of literature itself: if the Bible is saved, literature is immeasurably strengthened; though the Bible is a pearl of great price, literature itself is the chief affirmation of our very reason for being. Implicit in science's incapacity to deal with the Bible is science's incapacity to serve as an adequate guide to life. Implicit in the identified manner of the New Testament, that of accretive example, is a preference for practical, experiential revelation over philosophical disquisition. Analogous to Arnold's sense of religion—"*morality touched by emotion*"—is his sense of poetry—*ideas touched by feeling*. Even Arnold's purposiveness as a critic in *Literature and Dogma* has about it a parabolic character. His faith in the power of poetry, of literature, is immense. The role he assumes as a critic is to make the reader more totally available to this power—to its truth and its style, its idea and its feeling. But such power lies in the common accessibility of poetry, not in its mystery or unknowableness: like Arthur in Guinevere's final recognition, poetry is "the highest and most human too."

Therefore, Arnold does not attempt to bleed mystery into the common light of day, but to throw a "sunny white Light" on what is there for all to see. He is de-mystifying both "God" and the Bible. He is trying to bring our most common, universal, and practical sense of *conduct* to bear upon our most trustworthy guide and inspiration to conduct, the Bible. That is where its incomparable grandeur as literature resides: its "*morality touched by emotion*" (religion) as well as its *idea touched by feeling* (poetry). Centered in the high but common humanness of a universal faith experimentally verified, the Bible is centered in *us*, and it is Arnold's parabolic purpose, like Tennyson's purpose in *Idylls of the King*, to generate, through a renewed faith in the Bible, a renewed faith in ourselves.

This parabolic or analogical manner of Arnold's has the crucial effect of "placing" the critic in an organic rather than in a mechanical relationship to his literary object. It simultaneously activates and tests the critic's assumption that his object is one of the great embodiments of positive human experience by the criterion of perenniality, not of contemporaneity. A book looked at with uninhibited clarity for just what it is will, if it is truly great, reveal an insistent relevance to every age that honestly considers it. If it fails to do this, then either it is not one of the great books or the critic has failed to find its secret. But if a book passes these tests of authenticity and discovery, the critic will inevitably be deeply conscious of its pervasive relevance to his own time and will, consciously or unconsciously but irresistibly, shape his commentary in such a way as to reveal his double awareness of the book's distinctive character as a thing in itself as well as a book for all seasons.

And this relates to Arnold's use throughout his critical writings, including *Literature and Dogma*, of "human nature" as a persistent point of reference. There is in history an ever-shifting *Zeitgeist* which makes the cultural imperatives and availabilities of each epoch visibly different, and every great book, being shaped by the imperatives and availabilities of its *Zeitgeist*, is different in corresponding ways. But there is a sort of non-shifting, eternal *Zeitgeist*, too, rooted in those coordinates of man's basic nature which do not change. A great book is one that, despite the visible mark of its epoch, touches at a fundamental level these basic human coordinates. Such books, being perennially relevant, are perennially modern. Occasionally, however, "a favourable moment and the 'Zeit-Geist' " (276) make such a book quintessentially relevant and modern not only because the circumstances of the two ages reveal such numerous and metaphorically exact parallels but also because the original intuition which brought the book into being in the first place is thus so urgently needed by the later age.

This is the situation of the late nineteenth century regarding the Bible. Since, by Arnold's judgment, the late nineteenth century had the capacity to become an expansively critical age rather than an expansively creative one, the best the critic could do was to restore for his age the incomparable guidance of a great book that, though produced by another, was wholly relevant to it. The urgently needed act of literary redemption that provides the Arnoldian critic's central motive also shapes his critical method. *Literature and Dogma* is a superb example of a close, sensitive, imaginative reading of a redeemed literary text: it arrives at its explication of the Bible through a relentless attention to "how these words worked originally" (289). But it is superbly extra-textual too: it reads the needs of its original ages (c. 1000 B. C.–c. 100 A. D.) out of, not *into*, the text; it shows how later critical ages have read their needs *into* the text; and it shows how the present age more than anything else needs the original intuition of a Bible unadulterated by the *Aberglaube* of its own or subsequent ages.

But Arnold's critical extra-textuality neither moves the text off-center nor borrows from history, ancient or contemporary, one iota of literary justification or reinforcement. The eye of the critic is always on the original text, his evidence strictly internal. His abiding faith is in the text's own incomparable value. What he adds is a recognition of and zeal for literary usability: as a great book did not emerge from a vacuum, so its value cannot be vacuous. It is part of the critic's conscientious duty not to force-feed his intuition of a great book's greatness into a generation unfavorable to its reception, but to bring the power of the book and the power of his own time into organic concurrence when he recognizes "a favourable moment and the 'Zeit-Geist' " (276). It is at that moment a critic comes closest to performing a truly creative act, is at his furthest remove from dilettantism. To preserve the integrity of the text intact is a matter of honor, to make the text work for the largest possible number of readers is a matter of conscience. Without the extra-textuality which, in Arnold, surfaces as a parabolic or analogical manner, the critic accomplishes his mission in only a very partial way.

Arnold is attempting to get his reader to *read* the Bible again (and again) in the light of this new critical apprehension. He wants his own book to function as a way of renewing in the reader's experience a book with an immeasurably greater function. To prepare the way for and induce a great creative experience is the only real usefulness of criticism, individually or epochally. Thus Arnold's restrospective critical tendencies were not precious or nostalgic, but wholly realistic. If, as he had argued in "On the Modern Element in Literature," that is most modern which is most relevant, and if the greatest books are the greatest sustainers of the most dynamically affective human experience—experience that, like its language, is "fluid, passing, and literary" (152)—then the greatest books are the greatest sources of human fluidity, growth, organic creativity. They are not historical except in their accidents; in essence, they are eternal: never old, always new. Criticism rightly leads to that magnifying experience. However, to the degree that, like excessive rhetoric in poetry, it draws attention to itself rather than to affective access to its grand object, it is faulted and counterproductive.

Criticism is successful, then, not only when it gives a satisfactory sense of what a great book possesses in the way of experience, but also when it makes of a critic-reader contract a dependable promise that the kind of experience said to be in a great book will in fact be found there, so a reader induced to make himself available to the book's central experience will undergo in the process of reading and re-reading it a peculiar personal transformation. That is the critic's proper role, not as a substitute, but as trustworthy precursor and facilitator. The *creator* "modernizes" the book, not the critic; to try to make it contemporaneous in any literal sense is simply a confession of bad faith in the book's own authenticity. This is where the literary historian and the literary critic essentially differ: the historian assumes that there are historical reasons to justify interest in the book; the critic assumes, in addition, that a book worthy of our interest has transcended history. In this the critic is like the creator: the creator perceives the archetypal character of human events; the critic perceives the archetypal character of books.

Hence Arnold would have found the theory that a work of literature means only what the critic finds there very strange indeed, since that would place the critic higher than the creator in determining what literary (i.e., human) experience the reader would have. It was his experience of criticism that very few critics were equal to the challenges provided by the truly great creators. So he would have asked, at least, *what* critics of *what* meaning of *what* books? And he would have said of the criticism what Aristotle said of the creation: the *action* is of primary importance, not what we as readers *feel about* the action: it is the creator, not the critic, who puts the action there, in the first place and the last.

Arnold repeatedly cites Goethe's statement that "man never knows how anthropomorphic he is" (e.g., 242). This notion is a crucial clue to his detachment from that idealistic tradition of nineteenth-century literary endeavor which had been chiefly fueled by the German Romantic philosophers and men of letters, and which, in a fashion that fundamentally transformed it, had been channeled torrentially into England by Carlyle. But Carlyle was not a Romantic critic in even the pure sense that Coleridge was: in *Sartor Resartus*, Romanticism is carefully mutated by method, and Carlyle severely Englishes, that is, empiricizes, his Germanic inheritance. But Arnold was even less Romantic than Carlyle: he was reasonably sanguine, in his criticism, about human possibilities, but transcendence except in the very practical metaphoric sense was not a foundation-stone of his muted sanguinity.

His critical hope was at least as classical as it was Romantic, and his critical method was wholly classical. This commitment to classicisim enabled him to use Goethe as such a satisfying role-model, while it made him so uncomfortable with Carlyle even at his best that he diminished Carlyle's estimate of the German Romantics, and it determined his preference for Emerson over Carlyle. Translated to its practical function in *Literature and Dogma*, "man never knows how anthropomorphic he is" means that man is wholly anthropomorphic and that his best hope for getting in touch with useful reality is through personal morphology, through a purposive, systematic, and wholly organic self-renewal. Such a goal was preeminently classical, and in such classical works as Apuleius' *Transformations* and Ovid's *Metamorphoses* it had its chief literary testaments.

The Bible was simply the greatest, the most eloquent, the most intense literary embodiment of the idea by which man's moral metamorphosis could most profitably direct itself. In the Old Testament, this idea is summed up in the sentence "*O ye that love the Eternal, see that ye hate the thing which is evil! to him that ordereth his conversation right shall be shown the salvation of God*" (Psalm xcvii.10 [175]); in the New Testament, the idea is summed up in the sentence "*Let every one that nameth the name of Christ depart from iniquity!*" (2 Timothy ii.19 [175]). Thus Pagan classicism and Hebrew-Christian classicisim are brought together by Arnold in the spirit of a wholly empirical Modernism which has hopes for man that are completely rooted in experimental and verifiable assumptions and that looks to literary experience for the best aid toward their realization. If something has eroded during the hundred and more years since the publication of *Literature and Dogma*, it is not the critical method but the critical hope; in that case, it is not the value of Arnold that is in question, but the value of life itself.

Classical rather than Romantic, but still organic, Arnold is discovering and laying open the "ruling passion of the whole mind" of the Bible. He is pointing to the imaginative center by which all the parts gain coherence and through which—gradually, with many imperfections, and over a whole millenium—that imagination makes its final disclosure. What he is doing, then, was organic in a meaningful way with the inner history of the Bible itself.

As the initial intuition of the classical Bible of the golden age had been lost in the misguided, inferior, pseudo-scientific poetry *(Aberglaube)* of a much later antiquity, so Christ's mission was to restore that initial intuition by which, through the depth and intensity of its emotion, morality was enabled to rise into and become religion. That recovered intuition, victimized by the *Aberglaube* rampant at the time of its recovery, was again soon lost, and *Literature and Dogma* is an organicist critic's efforts to show his readers what that original intuition was and how they might personally recover it. Thus there is a pervasive suggestion in *Literature and Dogma* that the real, authentic Christianity has never really been active in our popular religion and that the modern world threatens to abandon it before it has ever been tried.

A chief key to Arnold's critical organicism is his emphasis on the indispensability of style—*style is the man*—to any breakthrough in the historical consciousness: "Jesus Christ's new and different way of putting things was the secret of his succeeding where the prophets failed"(219). This rather familiar conception gets stunning renewal through its application to Jesus since he was not a writer but a personal embodiment of style: style and the man meet uniquely in the life-style of Jesus, whose mildness, self-renunciation, and inwardness of teaching in no sense prevented him from fully accomplishing his labors. His was not the paralyzing inwardness of a latter-day Romantic but the catalyzing inwardness of the integrated classical moralist. Jesus is unique, too, in that he has a supreme extra-textual existence: he inspired one of the great written testaments to an imitable human rectitude. He is, however, the object, not of evangelistic comprehensiveness, but of evangelistic suggestiveness. He looms larger than all the writing about him; and his extra-textual existence, of which the New Testament accounts give only hints, is the center of his incomparable magnetism. The motive which he provided was not essentially his lessons, inspiring though they may be, but his example, which incited personal devotion as a steady, intense, world-wide motive. He was not a writer, though his life released the poetry in great men's souls. He was the strangest and most compelling of all humans, the hero of humility.

Literature and Dogma is as "scientific" as criticism can be without ceasing to be criticism. It is severely monitored empirically, turning upon what we actually know rather than upon what we would like to think we know, but it is kept responsibly critical, is not allowed, in the name of criticism, to abandon the purpose of criticism. It does not become, for example, capriciously philological in the interests of being or appearing to be scientific because at some point philology loses its critical uses and becomes strictly (i.e., scientifically) philological. But it does not beg the question on the more traditional literary side either: it does not become so Romantically mythic that it begs the question through an emotive transcendence of the question.

This suggests how far Arnold (and criticism) has traveled from the subjectivity of the prefaces of Wordsworth and the *Biographia Literaria* and the *Confessions of an Inquiring Spirit* of Coleridge: "we" has taken the place of "I," and issues are tested, not against incontrovertible autobiographical experience, but against the *common* experience, how men use language and what they mean by it. This is the method, not of the Romantics, but of Aristotle; it is the classical method of empirical criticism and practical philosophy with the broadest humanistic base that can be made properly to apply to such a subject. Arnold is careful not to let the confessional mode of nineteenth-century poetry invade his criticism but to let symbolic experience hold steady in the face even of the inevitable enchantments, in an age desperate for transcendence, of symbolic aspiration.

Arnold's emphasis on conduct ("Look up to God" means "Consult your Conscience," 175) runs directly counter to the tendency of philosophy in his time (for example, the Caird brothers) to separate religion and morality. Thus again, he sidesteps "abstruse reasoning" and keeps very close to the search for the good life—"righteousness"—staying clear of moral philosophy in the interests of moral intelligibility, simplicity, function. Thus his emphasis is throughout practical, empirical, knowable: the object (as distinct from the philosophical meaning or the theological-scientific "meaning") of religion is conduct (175–77). Hence he insists that religion and ethics are separable only at the *theoretical* level, but that this antithesis is "quite a false one " at the *practical* level.[4]

His emphasis on a functional criticism has a firm analogue here. Arnold was obviously capable of the most abstruse reasoning: his ability to draw down to their essentials the most abstruse reasonings of others proves this. But he was non-theoretical in his approach on very deliberate and purposive grounds. He never lost sight of the fact that literary criticism, however pleasurable it might be, was a secondary, not a primary, species of literary work. However well it was done, it could not be genuine unless it was serviceable to the literary experience provided by the creators, not by the critics. Hence, each of his works was an effort to enlarge the number of those equipped to profit internally from the finest literary experience. A theory of literature *per se* was likely to lose touch with the crucial object itself, to turn the reader's thoughts into "abstruse reasonings," and to become, finally, not a means, but an end. This he would have seen as self-defeating, however brilliant. Literature was too urgently needed by modern secular man to be sacrificed to a criticism that had become its own end.

Chapter V of *Literature and Dogma*—"The Proof from Miracles"—is especially rich in critical reverberations of the most fundamental sort. The requirement of the times is for a "new testament," and, as in all human history, that "new testament" is a literary testament, specifically here a revelation of the grand but purely human revelation of which the Bible is, in its particular field of attendance, an incomparable embodiment. Thus Arnold's approach to the Bible is a route of double access: by returning the Bible, through the rules and techniques of literary criticism, to its authentic status as a great work of literature, the critic not only makes the Bible function anew for the modern reader, but also enlarges the canon of great literature itself by firmly adding to it the greatest of all literary exemplifications of the human search for the good life through personal rectitude. Arnold recognizes the tendency of "men in general" to believe in miracles and to depend on them for authority: "It is almost impossible to exaggerate the proneness of the human mind to take miracles as evidence, and to seek for miracles as evidence . . ." (245); "Signs and wonders men's minds will have, and they create them honestly and naturally; yet not so but that we can see *how* they create them" (246).

Thus miracle-making and miracle-believing are much larger than the human experience embodied in the metaphysician's Bible, though they are conspicuous there. Arnold also delicately dismantles the textual "proof" for Biblical miracles, while emphasizing his belief that the emergent *Zeitgeist* will itself—"without insistence, without attack, without controversy" (257)—sap belief in miracles. Nor does Arnold show any enthusiasm for those mythic patternings, essentially anthropological in their significance, which move Biblical fable and character into an ultimately archetypal frame, patternings which would soon get their most dramatic presentation in the psychological theories of Jung. "Such speculations," says Arnold ironically, "almost take away the breath of a mere man of letters" (239). Even if valid in their own right and in degree true, they are not really germane to what literary experience, or a criticism that takes literary experience as its central object, is fundamentally concerned with. Though perhaps more valid than the historically held patterns they would replace, they draw literature toward metaphysical abstruseness, not toward the "facts of positive experience." Arnold thus draws a third element into his critical equation: to the ultimately unsustainable reliance on miracles for the Bible's authentic human workability and the overwhelming tendency of the human mind to seek out and use miracles as evidence, he adds the rapidly developing exploitation of the hypothesis of archetypal mythicism in the new "science" of anthropology.

Against all three of these, he sets a severe and enveloping classicism. Great literature is man's chief mechanism of salvation *in this world*, and it does its work, not by yielding to tendencies which it both recognizes and, at the same time, sees as humanly erosive, but by correcting them through a process that perpetually returns man to the "facts of positive experience" and perpetually tries to make him understand that his salvation is there or nowhere. Arnold's explicit application of this fundamental classicisim is to the Bible—both to Bible-writers who had yielded to the miraculous *Aberglaube* of their time and to later commentators who had exploited that capitulation to a miracle mentality.

But Arnold's fundamental classicisim has here a shorter-ranged implicit application too—namely, to the tendency of certain Romantic writers and critics so to mythicize human experience in their poetry and in their evaluations of poetry as to give to it a metaphysical rather than a positive experiential quality and to beat " 'in the void [their] luminous wings in vain.' "[5] The great classical writers, both Hebrew and Greek, had brought myth to the affective level of the human pulse-beat. Arnold saw the Romantic-Modern temptation not to hold steady in a faith in human actions, in "the facts of positive experience," but to respond to a hieratic sense of urgency by creating new mythic miracles detached from the human pulse-beat, as "availing nothing, effecting nothing." Such a response failed to correct a pervasive human tendency and, besides contributing to a delusion that must ultimately collapse with profound after-shocks, it missed the opportunity to contribute to human growth at a simple organic level. Moreover, it reinforced a Romantic disposition, with metaphysical overtones, to make of the poet an infallible seer and to strip him of that universal proneness to error which, once accepted, enlarges rather than diminishes his affectiveness with a modern reader to whom the very notion of infallibility has had to be abandoned.[6]

Chapter VI—"The New Testament Record"—moves even more steadily and confidently toward a revelation of the limitations of various schools of criticism and a full statement of the severe requisites of genuine literary criticism. One of its most rewarding moments (262ff.) is Arnold's identification of a central tension in the New Testament which is the dynamic source of dramatic excitement in all literature. The New Testament is literature made of literature (the New made of the Old), and a primary dimension of its *literary* experience is our involvement in a measuring of two readings of literature—Christ's reading and the reading of the New Testament writers—by which we clearly see the difference between a master-critic and critics with "a truer moral susceptiveness" than their countrymen but still crippled by imperatives of their *Zeitgeist*. This comparative process leads Arnold naturally to an identification and critique of the critical modes that his own century has applied to the same great testament of positive human experience, the Bible. Thus he is able to identify the chief dispositions of modern criticism and to measure them according to their relative success in unlocking the secret of the same literary document.

The least satisfactory, of course, have been *the metaphysical critics*. In their theological manifestation, they have simply built a house of falsehood around an intuition of truth and have put truth itself in danger of being lost to many people as their artificial invention crumbles around them. In their more modern mythic manifestation, they simply function under the false premise "that metaphysics should . . . always confer the superiority upon their possessor" (272). *The textual critics* simply do not have the data to settle their questions. Their case is, in any event, not essential to the kind of criticism most needed since even the most authentic primitive text would not erase the theurgy and thaumaturgy by which the New Testament writers were influenced and by which they obscured the intuition of Jesus. *The rationalistic critics*, on the other hand, are not authentically historical: they have "too narrow a conception of the history of the human mind, and of its diversities of operation and production" (269) and miss the mark by imposing contemporaneousness ("men rational in our sense and way") upon the past. *The historical critics* of the Bible have in general (Ewald is an exception, Baur, Strauss, and even Renan are not) attempted to settle by external evidence a problem—"what comes from Jesus" (270)—that requires internal evidence. This demands a higher degree of literary tact, a comparative method that is meticulously textual, a capacity for "right note-catching" that poets have always depended on in their best readers, than the historical critics have possessed or than their critical methodology has allowed them. Finally, *the philosophical critics*, though their contribution is real when they are genuinely philosophical, tend even at their best to translate "a great and free thought" into "a narrow and mechanical interpretation" (274).

As he rises to his climactic elaboration of the severe demands of a conscientious literary criticism against the background of criticism so often partial and inadequate, that is, criticism lamed by a restricting methodology or the peremptory *Aberglaube* of its age, Arnold cites two extraordinarily simple texts as monitoring the spirit of his criticism. The first is from Newton, and he calls it "the cardinal rule" of his critical inquiry: "*Hypotheses non fingo,*" *I do not invent [my] hypotheses* (275). The other is from the *Imitation,* and it is given as an example of a text providing its own best key to itself: "*Esto humilis et pacificus, et erit tecum Jesus!*" *Be humble and quiet, and Jesus will be with you* (275). The two texts taken together are stunningly illuminative of Arnold's critical organicism: when science reaches toward poetry and conduct toward perfection, criticism invokes its genuine muse.

Arnold's critical method is one of "intuition and practical rule"(298), and he saw compelling analogies for such a method in both Aristotle and Jesus as critics of literature. Aristotle, he says, "does not appeal to a speculative theory of the system of things, and deduce conclusions from it" (296). Rather, Aristotle recognized that "the law of our being is *not* something which is already definitively known" but "something which discovers itself and *becomes*" the law of our being (296). Thus Aristotle, like Arnold, depended rather upon "the experience [that] is ripe and solid, and to be used safely, long before the theory" (297). However "beautiful and impressive" a theory may be, whether of aesthetics or of ethics, it resists a reduction to experience and to that degree becomes relatively trivial and dysfunctional. Theory places emphasis on how a doctrine was reached, not on the doctrine itself. It is inorganic except within the system in which it has a place. Jesus, like Aristotle, dealt with experience that was "ripe and solid," and, like Aristotle, he was attentive to organic becoming: "How he reached a doctrine we cannot say; but he always exhibited it as an intuition and practical rule, and a practical rule which, if adopted, would have the force of an intuition for its adopter also" (297–98).

Arnold's perception of Jesus as a great student of letters, as an organicist literary critic, is a dramatic dimension of his whole effort to humanize the Bible. By "restoring the intuition," Jesus was returning men's awareness to the initial and authentic spirit of the Old Testament. He dealt in language, moved his disciples by freeing language from the encrustations of *Aberglaube* into which the original intuition of the classical Hebrews had been imprisoned by their then modern successors. He made the words of the Old Testament work differently from the way they worked in the theological rigidities of Jewish orthodoxy.

Thus Jesus "was for ever translating [*Aberglaube*] into the sense of the higher ideal, the only sense in which it had truth and grandeur" (305). He used words in a special way (305), had an intuitive preference for certain words out of the Old Testament (308), and he was the most practical, the least theoretical, of the critics of the Old Testament (208), ultimately resting his revelation on the most practical rule of all: "*Follow me!*" He was, of course, a great literary creator too, his great *secret* (inwardness) and his great *method* (self-renunciation) working through his great *style* (felicity) to produce "the total impression of his 'epieikeia,' or sweet reasonableness . . ." (300). He came to possess this incomparable genius for conduct, this wholly practical, processive, experiential insight into the human way to permanent happiness, by doing what the modern literary critic must do—by following Scripture "continuously and interpreting it naturally" (281) and thereby recovering the original, indispensable intuition of Israel—by conscientiously caring and conscientiously attending (288). Jesus exceeded the role of literary critic and became a great literary founder, not only by rubbing the dust off the clichés into which the original intuition of the Old Testament had fallen, but also by creating a new voice, a new language and imagery, that makes his insight exact and permanent beyond measure of any other.

Chapter IX—"*Aberglaube* Re-Invading"—is one of those broad historical sweeps (c. 100 – c. 1873) which Arnold did so confidently and which "scientific" critics and "scientific" historians and "scientific" theologians are most impatient with and tend most to slur. Although it is untenable as history, it is just as surely irresistible as emblematic critical narrative. There can be no doubt about the meaning of his term *Aberglaube;* and there can be no doubt that a mentality suggested by that metaphor took hold of Christianity during this period of "almost two thousand years" or that it was largely alien to the original intuition of the Old Testament and the recovered intuition of the New. The account of the progressive hardening of the official Creeds (Apostles', Nicene, Athanasian) is persuasive enough, and the comparison of the Psalms with the *Soliloquies* of St. Augustine is a brilliantly effective critical strategy.

To attempt what Arnold attempts in thirty pages, or even in three thousand is, in one sense, absurd. Nevertheless, it is also astounding how much "tact, measure, and correct perception" (361) he shows in moving so rapidly among the various pressure points of medieval Christianity; in distinguishing between the centers of gravity in post-Reformation Protestantism and Catholicism; in identifying the recognizable physiognomy of contemporary Evangelicalism with the fairy-tale of the three Lord Shaftesburys; and in yet defending the innate humanness of this untenable popular science of religion against the charge of his "philosophical Liberal friends" that it is all " 'a degrading superstition.' " Though it is necessarily extra-textual in a rather grand way, the Biblical text from which it is a bursting release is now securely in place. This, together with the critical manner of the chapter itself, suggests that representative Patristic, Scholastic, and Reformation documents are fresh in Arnold's mind and are specifically monitoring the movement of his critical thought. So while one may readily concede that the chapter is in considerable degree an intuitive shot in the dark, he can still hold that it serves even the conscientious critic's overall purpose not only aptly but brilliantly. It is an organically rooted celebration of the discovery which the preceding chapters have enacted, and the discursiveness which invokes our historical skepticism is wrapped in a spirit of justified critical jubilee that largely erases our doubts.

Chapter X—"Our 'Masses' and the Bible"—is one of the most brilliantly and engagingly strategic chapters in *Literature and Dogma*. It contains the central "social idea" of the volume: it is past time for toying with "*the masses*"—they will have it straight or not at all. Since they, like all of us, need an adequate guide to right conduct, and since without such a guide their actions are likely to be anarchical, it behooves us to save the Bible if we would save social order. Although this puts the case in its extreme social form, it is the underlying social intuition of Arnold's book.

Such a formulation enables us to pinpoint the audience of

Literature and Dogma. Neither the masses themselves nor the professional exponents of popular scientific religion are the plaintiffs and defendants in the case. Rather, Arnold's audience is the jury of the present who may, if they will, shape the future. They are those members of a society in rapid transition who are both conscientious and sensible, who are accessible to ideas, however unusual, that have self-evident relevance to their times, who are not blinded by the fanaticism of reform and know, therefore, how to help ideas along without rushing to institutionalize them, and yet who have some experience and power of working toward improved social felicity without the visionary violence of utopianists. These are the readers to whom Arnold appeals, and his keen consciousness of them shapes his points of reference and critical methodology. Thus his appeal is essentially social and his criteria essentially empirical.

In the background is the figure and career of John Henry Newman, who had, a generation earlier, caught the attention and enthusiasm of clusters of this same audience and from whom, considering the similarities in their subject matter, Arnold has to distance himself as to both method and purpose. Newman had accepted (even restored) Revelation in its traditional ecclesiastical sense and had deduced his religious insights from it; Arnold reinterprets and humanizes the very idea of Biblical revelation and anchors it in wholly verifiable experience, strips it of syllogistic deduction, and subjects it to inductive experiment. Newman had insisted upon the distinction between *natural* and *revealed* religion; Arnold erases the distinction as ultimately unverifiable, since the "Great Personal First Cause" is common to them both. Newman's quarrel with Butler's *Analogy* Arnold sees as an archetypal contention irreconcilable on Newman's and Butler's terms, but he shows that it proceeds on a "line of hypothesis and inference" that "falls to pieces like a house of cards" (366) once the hypothesis is withdrawn.

The anthropomorphism from which both Butler and Newman would save religion Arnold sees as one of man's saving remnants in matters of religion ("*Man . . . never knows how anthropomorphic he is,*" 242). Although anthropomorphism may lead him, under the influence of abstraction-merchants, to "metaphysical ideas of the personality of God" (368), such ideas are only the natural extravagances of his "anthropomorphic language," and his anthropomorphism ultimately leads him back to the humanly verifiable, to experience, to "plain experimental proof" (366). By *trying* it, that is, by experiment, he will find that personal rectitude is the true source of happiness or peace. By comparing the various guides to rectitude, that is, by *trying* them, he will find that the Bible is incomparably the best guide. Having had the actual experience of the joy that comes of right conduct, having actually had his *morality touched by emotion,* he will be immune to the notional religion of even such an "exquisite and delicate genius" as Dr. Newman (377). Thus Arnold's *Literature and Dogma* is a wholly different "grammar of assent" from Newman's, and part of his purpose is to set in reverse motion Newman's whole idea of "the development of Christian doctrine."

Finally, Arnold's audience is one that would be rather easily persuaded that the age of the *homo unius libri,* the man of one book, is over, that times do change, and that their best guides to the future are a sensitivity to the " 'Zeit-geist' and a prolonged and large experience of men's expressions and how they employ them . . ." (373). Newman's disqualifiction was not in the latter, but in the former: he had been born into the world twenty years too soon and had not been "touched with the breath of the 'Zeit-Geist' " now everywhere abroad. So the widest reading and the most "exquisite and delicate genius" are not enough, nor is impeccable conscientiousness. One must know, in addition, "the history of the human spirit and its deliverances" (378) and that "*Time. . . , the wisest of all things, . . . is the unfailing discoverer*" (265).

In the end, Arnold holds steady in his faith in Israel's idea, in the method he has employed in unlocking that idea, and in the ultimate victory of that idea if man would survive. But he recognizes, too, that neither his method nor Israel's idea will dominate the short curve of the future. More chaos and more Catholicism are likely to have their day first, but as "the whole career of the human race" (386) fulfills, in Aristotle's words, the law of its being, Israel's prophecy will be fulfilled. In the meantime, one's chief work is to show that the true religion of Israel is "incomparably higher, grander, more wide and deep-reaching, than the *Aberglaube* and false science which it displaces" (384–85). One's chief consolation is, in the words of Newman's Oriel compeer Davison, that " 'Conscience and the present constitution of things are not corresponding terms; it is conscience and the issue of things which go together' " (386). *En passant*, Arnold begs the utmost indulgence for popular religion, utmost disdain for learned religion, and shows, with witty elegance, how the centers of European culture, from ancient Greece to modern France, Italy, and Germany, have attempted to sidestep the prophetic idea of Israel and said rather, with Abraham, " 'Oh that Ishmael might live before thee!' " (389).

The future of Christianity cannot be prophesied simply because, in its authentic fullness, it has never been tried: we have not yet had full experience of it. Christianity itself, impeded almost from the beginning by the *Aberglaube* of orthodoxy, has "brought the world . . . *to regard righteousness, as only the Jews regarded it before the coming of Christ*" (398). We have had a great *show* of Christianity, but very little reality of it. Indeed our situation is closely analogous to Christ's situation, and we have had corresponding impediments to a genuine practice of his way. Never having practiced Christianity, we cannot testify to its effects on the basis of experimental proof. We have such metaphysical notions of immortality because we have not typed in ourselves the experience by which life's victory over death can be experimentally known. But the Jesus of the New Testament can persuade us of "the infinite" of Christianity—"its immense capacity for ceaseless progress and farther development"(405)—if we can be shown that it is in fact in the Bible (*the work of literary criticism*) and if we will read and re-read "the gospels continually, until we catch something of it" (*the work of literature itself*).

In the "Preface" to the first edition, Arnold states as his fundamental purpose "to find, for the Bible, . . . a basis in something that can be verified, instead of in something which has to be assumed" (150). He realizes that, to do this, he will have "to recast religion" (150), but he realizes, too, that the time is not only right but imperative if the Bible and the Bible-religion are to be saved. The *Zeitgeist* has suffused modern life with "some notion of the processes of the experimental sciences," and people are now everywhere demanding the "*ground* and *authority*" for religion's assertions.

But neither theological science nor physical science is equipped to deal with this demand because they do not have the proper intellectual equipment, the technique, or the experience to "watch the God of the Bible, and the salvation of the Bible, gradually and on an immense scale discovering themselves and *becoming* . . ." (152). This is culture's task, for only culture places the highest premium on "*getting the power, through reading, to estimate the proportion and relation in what we read*" (153). Only culture, the organic, processive result of wide, deep, repetitive reading, reading undertaken with the serious and systematic purpose of getting to know the best that has been thought and known in human history, prepares one to perceive the power, the crux, the distinctiveness of what one reads. Otherwise (especially if one has scant reading and an overabundance of scientific methodology), one reads to little purpose, missing the true "*ground* and *authority*" of what he does read. Theology is a proven failure; physical science is alienated from both the subject and the medium in which the subject subsists; knowledge, even the massive knowledge of Germany, leaves the central issue untouched or touches it only negatively.

What is needed is a wholly constructive literary criticism, and for this only culture of the widest, deepest, most experientially strengthened sort is a fit preparation since only culture, working through a large, rich, deep, imaginative mind, can produce a sufficiently keen and delicate instrument—*tact*. *Tact* is the most crucial critical term in the Arnold lexicon, and its presence in a critical endeavor separates the finest from the second-class, is the true "note" of the genuine critic. It comes, "in a clear and fair mind, from a wide experience" (157), and it expresses itself through "justness of perception" (158), "quickness and sureness of perception" (159). It is "quick" and "keen" and shows a "practical dexterity of perception," a fine and practical critical sureness. Tact leads the critic to "a true . . . sense of relative value" (160), identifies "intrinsic worth" (160), goes straight to the "internal evidence" (161), makes sound discriminations (161). Arnold does not define the term *tact* more specifically than this, but it is clear that, at the height of his power and experience as a literary critic, he considered tact the indespensable quality of any sound criticism or of any true culture. The fact that it is not a scientific term does not mean that the critical quality conveyed by it is either vague or insubstantial.

Tact is to Arnold's criticism what *inscape* is to Hopkins's aesthetics—that individually distinctive capacity to perceive the individually distinctive character of the object scrutinized. It is the literary critic's spiritual eye, by which he can recover a writer's original intuition and distinguish it from all other intuitions, can perceive justly and surely the total impression into which a writer's secret and method are converted by his style. This obviously is not an easily acquired capacity, but it seems to be worth all the literary experience, all of the observation, meditation, and imagination applied with systematic seriousness to the world's great books, necessary to acquire it. At least this much seems likely enough: that none but the most serious and purposeful students of literary experience can hope to acquire it, and that the world of literary experience itself would be vastly poorer without it.

Thus the three fundamental theses of this essay bear a consequential relationship: (1) that Arnold is solid and salutary for our time, still our sanest and most constructive literary voice because (2) he brought the critical act so close to the creative act that criticism's generative analogue is clearly visible in the creative work itself (3) through a critical organicism that perceives language, thought, and action as organic in a most various human nature, human nature as organic in a most various human history, and the world's great books as the supreme literary intuitions by which, individually, a magnificently gifted creator makes an inductive leap through his own *Zeitgeist* into the enveloping metaphor in which the *Zeitgeist* itself subsists.

To become available to these supreme literary intuitions, the critic must himself undergo an organic transformation for which a deep, wide, and oft-repeated experience of the world's greatest books is the only affective method. If, like the poet, he would lend out to others a mind thus transformed, he must, again by analogy with the poet, always prefer the great book to himself, being most successful when he most fully succeeds in effacing himself and allowing the great book to subsist as it did (and does) in nature. And the contemporary student of literature who begins to understand Arnold's superb, dynamic critical organicism cannot conscientiously deny his persistent and massive relevance to the art of criticism. He may chafe at it, rail at it, insult it, hate it. But if he is a serious, gifted, purposive student of literature, he will end "by receiving its influence and by undergoing its law."

NOTES

1. "The Victorian Imagination: A Nonpolemical Introduction," in *The Victorian Imagination: Essays in Aesthetic Exploration* (New York: New York University Press, 1980), pp. 10–11. See also pp. 11–13 for further elaboration of this point of view.
2. All references to *Literature and Dogma* are to *The Complete Prose Works of Matthew Arnold*, ed. R. H. Super (Ann Arbor: University of Michigan Press, 1968), VI, and page references are given in parentheses in the text.

   Perhaps it is unnecessary to remark that this essay deals strictly with Arnold's method as a critic of *literature* and does not invade the fascinating questions of Arnold's religion or of his place in the evolution of modern Biblical studies, about both of which there is a substantial corpus of commentary and the need for a good deal more.
3. "Moral" in Arnold has Aristotelian rather than apothegmatical significance.
4. Carlyle had developed this point in considerable detail and to an analogous end in "The Hero as Poet."
5. "Shelley," in *Essays in Criticism, Second Series, Complete Prose Works*, ed. Super (1977), XI, 327.
6. Throughout *On Heroes, Hero-Worship and the Heroic in History*, Carlyle had reiterated this creative distinction between human perfection and human grandeur. See especially "The Hero as Prophet" and "The Hero as King."

The Poetics of Matthew Arnold's Prose

Essays in Criticism

One of the distinct advantages of the organization of R. H. Super's superb edition of *The Complete Prose Works of Matthew Arnold*[1] is that it enables us, without any reorganizational effort of our own, to look at Arnold's works from another side. If we are familiar with *Essays in Criticism, First Series* only as the content and order were fixed after the third edition of 1875, for example, we cannot, even if we know all the facts, so easily witness the process by which the product evolved as we can by reading the third volume of Professor Super's edition, with its critical, explanatory, and textual notes.

In *Lectures and Essays in Criticism,* we can better follow the whole story—the order of composition, essays vs. lectures-cum-essays, rejections, adaptations, emendations, revisions. We can get very close to the emergence of the book in Arnold's own mind: to the order in which his thoughts and analogies surfaced; the part one or more essays played in affecting the subject matter and frame of reference of other essays considered individually or collectively; the point at which Arnold's critical consciousness took a strategic leap from primary emphasis on the life, literary work, and defining character of an individual to the life, literary work, and defining character of an epoch; the care with which he strove to maintain this startlingly enlarged sense of the critic's role in modern life while preserving the critic's essential literary rootedness. Obviously, this closeness makes a tremendous difference to anyone who wants to be as precise as possible in his critical measurings, to anyone who thinks that evidence bearing significantly on the decisions, conscious or unconscious, by which an author ultimately established a classic literary text is valuable. One need not agree unreservedly with Herbert Paul's statement that it is "Mr. Arnold's most important book in prose, the central book, so to speak, of his life"[2] to perceive *Essays in Criticism, First Series* as a classic literary text.[3]

The book itself is not changed: the *Essays in Criticism* of which Arnold fixed the content and order in 1875 is the same *Essays in Criticism* that all readers since then have held in their hands and will hold in their hands in the future. What Professor Super's reordering of the individual essays[4] does is alter in fundamental ways reader perspective on the book. It changes our perception of the process by which the book developed—by a method that is predominantly inductive and exploratory rather than predominantly deductive and syllogistic, providing enlarged if implicit bases for judging the self-criticism to which Arnold subjected his work, excluding some pieces and pillaging some to strengthen others, and making more visible the indispensable part self-criticism plays in Arnold's overall critical programme. It reveals a new degree of tension, a new degree of critical dynamism, in the book by dissolving a single imperious order and, through a reminder that it is "the business of criticism to deal with every independent work as with an independent whole" (174), frees each essay to challenge, in our evaluative minds, the predominant place in the volume of "The Function of Criticism at the Present Time" or "The Literary Influence of Academies." By its insistence that we give greater attention to the autonomy of the individual essays, following the direct, internal evidence of each to its separate center, it clarifies and magnifies the book as a whole, making a good deal clearer and more impressive the degree to which Arnold has established connections between his primary subject, criticism, and philosophy, religion, and the practical ethics of a timeless moralist tradition. Through his value-metaphor of a "free play of the mind upon all subjects" as an object of desire, its realization being one of the most exquisite pleasures of civilized man (268), Arnold has put philosophy, religious experience, and the finer conceptions of morality at the service of criticism in a uniquely integral way.

Looking at the book from another side does not, of course, mean looking at it from that side only. Its value is as a critical addition, not as a critical substitute. If the new way of looking at the book has validity, it will release a flow of fresh knowledge without which criticism of even an undeniably important book becomes repetitive and, ultimately, inert. But its permanent value will be inherent chiefly in the new critical synthesis which results from the necessary accommodation of habitual perspectives to a fresh viewpoint and the critical interest which that process of accommodation generates.

The history of Arnold's impact on the critical enterprise during the last hundred years is, in its principal outlines, clear enough. He was, quite simply, the founder of the main line of modern criticism in English. During the 1860s and 1870s, he gave criticism an identity, a broad-based cultural complexity and intellectual respectability, and a social mission that was both modern and indispensable. He released criticism from the college and the coterie, endowing it, not with a definition, but with a character, a profoundly felt, multi-dimensional creative presence with the power to touch people into life. He did nothing to trigger odious, self-defeating comparisons, and such comparisons have as little value now as they have ever had. He was thoroughly respectful of Johnson, Burke, and Coleridge, for example, and he did what he could to bring them to the attention of a generation that had forgotten them. But something far more basic than restoring even worthy icons to their rightful niche was needed by a generation that could confuse the importance of Bishop Colenso with the importance of Martin Luther (278). Carlyle, Mill, and Ruskin were voices heard in the land, but Carlyle, partly as a result of the astigmatism brought on by his disproportionate view of the German Romantics (108), had misread the future, and his critical usefulness had been greatly diminished by the furious falsetto of the *Latter-Day Pamphlets* (275). Mill was "a writer of distinguished mark and influence, a writer deserving all attention and respect" (136), who suffered by the measure of one of his own maxims—the good is often the enemy of the best. When Ruskin turned from aesthetics to political economy, he lost such hold as he had had on a whole generation of readers (275). So the power of Arnold was just the power his moment needed.

The function of Arnold's criticism was, as has already been hinted and as will be developed more fully later in this essay, essentially a creative function: to give people a sense of being alive not dependent on the senses, while reminding them that, though their generation was not producing great books, the great books of the past were wholly relevant to their need for intellectual, moral, spiritual, and aesthetic nurture. In truth, despite the dust of controversy that his matter and his manner stirred up, his impact on the younger writers of the period was just what he hoped it would be. Swinburne, Pater, and Hardy were among those who owed Arnold a considerable creative debt. But in the generation or so between Arnold's death and T. S. Eliot's majority, Arnold's legacy fell into the hands of some rather dull disciples, as not infrequently happens. When Eliot began his career as a poet-critic, Arnoldianism was in a state somewhat comparable to the state in which Arnold had himself found Romanticism in the 1840s and 50s. It was no part of Eliot's mission to restore Arnoldianism to its best self, as it had not been Arnold's mission to restore Romanticism. So Eliot built a critical edifice that, while it was hugely indebted to Arnold, embodied a running quarrel with him.

Arnold persisted on his own merits as the central touchstone of academic criticism in both England and America, and individual creative spirits still looked to him for guidance. Eliot, however, had effectively weaned the avant-garde from Arnold in America, and no leading critic since Eliot, including Trilling, has shown even Eliot's somewhat grudging understanding of the fundamentally *creative* thrust of Arnold's criticism.[5] The young Trilling wrote the best critique[6] of a generation fast losing contact with an Arnold, who, while he has larger relevance to the last quarter of the twentieth century than any other critic in English, past or present, was so sensitive to his moment in time that he chose his metaphors, structured his thoughts, and designed his strategies with very particular reference to its nuances and needs. The later Trilling, except in some vaguely analogous sense, was not essentially Arnoldian at all.

Setting aside studies of special topics like those by Faverty, Robbins, and Sells,[7] general commentary on Arnold's critical prose since Eliot and Trilling has been somewhat miscellaneous: intellectually confused like Brown's,[8] willfully hostile like James's,[9] sympathetic but fidgety like Tillotson's,[10] or rigid and ponderous like Madden's.[11] As a result, the Arnold of the commentators has, over the years, seemed less and less relevant, and there have been recent calls for a fundamental re-examination of the primary critical Arnold.[12]

If what has been said above about altered reader perspective on *Essays in Criticism* is true, then it is fair to see the book as belonging to an order of creativity in the literary art that is more encompassing than literary criticism as ordinarily conceived (or even as such), to see Arnold's explicit efforts to enlarge the field and to clarify and deepen the function of literary criticism as resulting, perhaps inevitably, in the creation of an imaginative structure or literary text that far exceeds its central working metaphor and reaches, rather in the manner of poetry, toward life itself in one of its representative aspects. Indeed, the fairness of this view of the book is strongly reinforced by the cluster of literary associations and connections that the very articulation of this view triggers in the critical consciousness. It becomes almost spontaneously clear, for example, that Arnold's famous characterizations of poetry as "*a criticism of life*" and "the application of ideas to life" have *prima facie* relevance to *Essays in Criticism*, not just as discursive ideas promulgated by the book, but, again in the manner of poetry, as imaginative processes which we as readers witness and in which we participate at an experiential level that is deeper and more affective than mere intellectual participation. As in poetry, our faith, value-systems, and idealistic aspirations become involved.

At the point when we surmise that the central working metaphor of the book is not only topical (a critical way of looking at literature) but also mythic (a critical way of looking at life), it also becomes instantly clear that it could hardly be otherwise. Inherent in Arnold's view that literature is a people's most authentic way of telling, intentionally or unintentionally, the real truth about themselves is the hypothesis that, in dealing with literature (its specialized topic), criticism is necessarily dealing with life (its mythic or humanistic object, both its motive and its goal). This recognition leads in turn, for the practiced student of literary phenomena, to certain inevitable questions of a slightly more specialized or professional kind. Were there other books in the background of *Essays in Criticism* that were attempting, with different working metaphors, to do the same sort of thing? Were there reasons for Arnold's dissatisfaction with their achievement along a comparable line of endeavor? What, by comparison with them, are the differences in Arnold's value-assumptions and literary strategies, in his matter and manner?

In a general but very real sense, of course, the whole Western literary tradition lies in the background of Arnold's book, and the critical postures of Plato, Aristotle, Saint Francis of Assisi, Shakespeare, Spinoza, Goethe, for example—their distinctive ways of looking at and thinking about life—have specific, demonstrable relevance to what is going on in *Essays in Criticism*. Their hypotheses, the way they played their literary roles, their sense of themselves in relation to their world monitor the book in both a positive and a negative way.[13] But, as has been suggested, Arnold's metaphors, like the metaphors of the poets whom he admired, radiate outwards from specificity, not inward from vagueness. In both his poetry and his prose, he perpetually stalked his own era's *Zeitgeist*, identifying its details with great particularity and subjecting it to the test of literary representation with relentless persistence. "*Time*," he said in *Literature and Dogma*, "*Time—, the wisest of all things,—is the unfailing discoverer*."[14]

Thus the phrase "at the Present Time" in the title of his introductory essay is a signal, not of temporal provincialism, but of imaginative or poetic method. The only chance given us to understand with some degree of solidity the truth about the human condition, about man's responses and prospects, his place in nature, is that of looking with uninhibited clarity at one's own moment in time because that is the only direct experience of life in this world that we will ever have, the only "fact" or "truth" available for conversion to a more encompassing order of significance. To "see things as they *in fact* are" (emphasis added) does not imprison us in a meaningless infinity of details (a wholly unimaginative state), but, except perhaps for the mystic, the fantasist, or the madman, it is the indispensable base upon which the critical imagination builds, creating meaning rather than imagining "facts."

Arnold made a supreme effort to see the facts of life in his contemporary world for himself and to represent them distinctively and meaningfully for his readers. But, like poets especially and men of letters generally, he had a keen, a self-formative interest in the literary representations of others. *Essays in Criticism* is, indeed, literature made of literature, and criticism is the working metaphor for its technique of transmutation. The ultimate function of criticism is creativity. Epochally considered, it is the indispensable precursor, preparing the way for a supreme moment of poetic revelation, cultivating an ambience in which the bearers of the highest order of insight, the poets, can fully realize their creative talent.

However, the individual is not just the servant of the future. He can realize in himself, in miniature as it were, the critical-creative process that, in its epochal dimensions, involves several generations. Through a genuinely critical habit of mind, the individual can purify and clarify his perceptual world to the degree necessary to release in himself such a climax of creativity as he, individually, is capable of. This is the poetic result realized by the chief *personae* of Arnold's book: the Guérins, Heine, Marcus Aurelius, Spinoza, Joubert. They are not models of human perfection, but they are, perceived in the oblique manner of poetry, humanity's heroes: human beings tried much as others, including ourselves, are tried, but managing nonetheless to realize a goodly portion of their human potential and, by looking at themselves and their world honestly, respectfully, and idiosyncratically, to achieve at least recurrent moments of creative vision. They did not *do* anything spectacular, yet they *became* something both extraordinary and wholly accessible to us all. In that specific sense, Arnold's *Essays in Criticism* can be seen as lightly but consciously counterpointing Carlyle's *Heroes, Hero-Worship and the Heroic in History*. Moreover,

Arnold seems to have looked at three other literary representations having relevance to contemporary life—Carlyle's *Past and Present*, Newman's *The Idea of a University*, Mill's *On Liberty*—and to have seen his own book as corrective of rather than in contention with them.

Arnold refers to Carlyle in only a few places in the book, and he makes no direct reference to *Past and Present*. Further, Arnold's views of Carlyle, which seem always to have been ambivalent, are, in 1863–1864, rather retrospective: in his earlier period, Carlyle misconstrued the importance of the German Romantics (107–08); in his later period, he diminished his usefulness by his "furious raid" into "political practice" (275). Carlyle had not, therefore, been a wholly trustworthy critic, lacking "justness of spirit" and the capacity to "ascertain the master-current in the literature of an epoch" (107) and revealing, despite his very great ability, the distortions of an extravagant spirit through the metaphor of an extravagant prose style (247). That Arnold had *Past and Present* particularly in mind is suggested by the fact that it is, after *Sartor Resartus*, Carlyle's most Romantic text, the reflection of a spiritual tendency that had led to his thorough misapprehension of Heine, who destroyed "that romantic school" (108), and by the fact that *Past and Present* is at the center of the nineteenth-century capitulation to Medievalism, by which Heine was not diverted from a true modernism, though he too felt "the fascinating power of the Middle Age" (119). In most of its important respects, Carlyle's *Past and Present* is antithetical to *Essays in Criticism* as a critical perspective on life for the generation Arnold is addressing: its Romantic version of idealism, the primacy it gives to a doctrine of action, its recurrence to the Middle Ages for its chief spiritual reference point, a charismatic extravagance of style that still echoes at a distance the subjectivity of the German Romantics and, by making prose do the work of poetry too transparently, cripples its function as prose.

The references to Newman in *Essays in Criticism* are even fewer than those to Carlyle, and again there is no direct reference to *The Idea of a University*. But there is the suggestion of something very like reverential awe in the language with which Arnold speaks of Newman: nobility (44), "*urbanity,*" "genius," "charm," "ineffable sentiment" (244), "a miracle of intellectual delicacy" (250). He takes from Newman's *Apologia* "an expression . . . which seems . . . fitted to be of general service; the *note* of so and so, the note of catholicity, the note of antiquity, the note of sanctity, and so on" (244). It is one of those points at which both the sensibilities and the intellectual interests of Newman and Arnold meet, and capturing the peculiar tone and vibration—the special mental and spiritual constitution—of *personae* who embody subtly differentiated responses to one or more of the philosophical, moral, religious, and aesthetic pressures of an alternative modernism is one fit way of describing what Arnold is attempting to do in *Essays in Criticism*.

The commonalty of substantive concerns between *The Idea of a University* and *Essays in Criticism* is clear to anyone who has read the two books. Seeing things as they in fact are is the reiterated insistence of both, as is the importance of distinguishing the real from the popular meaning of the terms of discourse. Both have conspicuous classical roots. In addition, Arnold's description of the nature and function of criticism, especially its transformational capacity and its ideal cultural result, reads like a variation on Newman's chapter entitled "Knowledge Its Own End." But despite their intellectual harmony and mutually supportive sympathies, they are very different books. *Essays in Criticism* may be seen as corrective of *The Idea of a University* because Arnold's book, by virtue of its *treatment* of a subject in many ways comparable to Newman's, is more culturally conversional, less purely theoretical, and, through its extensive use of the biographical mode, humanizes its subject and makes it more accessible to the daily life of the reader. In that sense, *Essays in Criticism* is a far more poetic book than *The Idea of a University.* The contrast between Newman's method of supremely impressive but severely detached discourse and Arnold's method of involvement, of implanting in the imagination of the reader an implicit design that is working at a subliminal level not significantly touched by argument *per se,* is an indication of the presence in Arnold's prose of a large poetic element and a useful suggestion of how that poetic element is to be critically viewed.

Language as metaphor has a narrative as well as a philosophical significance in Arnold's prose: historical narrative is interwoven with personal narrative in the acculturation and humanization of argument. The imaginative design reveals that what Arnold appears to be doing superbly well explicitly is really only a metaphor of what he is doing implicitly. It is to this quality that Arnold seems to have been pointing when, on re-reading the essays, he said that he was "struck by the admirable riches of human nature that are brought to light in the group of persons of whom they treat, and the sort of unity that as a book to stimulate the better humanity in us the volume has."[15] Orchestration and celebration of a purely humanistic, secular kind are more conspicuous goals of *Essays in Criticism* than of *The Idea of a University*, which Arnold finds ways of achieving with less offense to the classic proprieties of prose than did Carlyle.

Arnold begins his essay on "Marcus Aurelius" with a direct reference to Mill's *On Liberty*. He cites Mill's dismissive attitude toward Christian morality, that Christian morality, "in certain most important respects . . . 'falls far below the best morality of the ancients' " (132), and then shows that, unless one judges moralists on the basis simply of the sincere, rational way in which they elaborate their moral arguments (135–36), as Mill had in fact done in *On Liberty*, this position is untenable. Drawing contrasting examples from the *Imitation* and from the Old and New Testaments, on the one hand, and from Epictetus, on the other, Arnold demonstrates the affective superiority of the Christian moralists in their having "supplied the emotion and inspiration" necessary to carry one into the moral stream, in their having "*lighted up* morality" (134). In short, the Christian moralists have not been better philosophers; they have been better poets, and that is the proper measure of their affective superiority over the pagan moralists. Arnold then rounds off his direct attention to Mill and *On Liberty* as follows:

> It is because Mr. Mill has attained to the perception of truths of this nature, that he is,—instead of being, like the school from which he proceeds, doomed to sterility,—a writer of distinguished mark and

influence, a writer deserving all attention and respect; it is (I must be pardoned for saying) because he is not sufficiently leavened with them, that he falls just short of being a great writer."(136)

It is the deftest possible criticism, giving Mill everything he deserves and not an iota more, while at the same time saving the Christian moralist tradition from the rough handling of one not quite qualified, as judged by the tests he applies, to deal with it justly. Mill is a distinguished rationalist philosopher with an unusually keen aesthetic sense. But, ironically, Mill's aesthetic sense is "negative rather than positive, passive rather than active,"[16] and he is neither Christian enough nor poet enough to be an adequate critic of Christian morality.

At this point, Arnold seems to set Mill aside and to deal exclusively with Marcus Aurelius. The truth is, however, that he never takes his eye off Mill during the course of the essay. The subliminal measuring to which he subjects Mill and the Utilitarians is a key to the imaginative design of the piece and, through imaginative design, to its poetics.

At the heart of "Marcus Aurelius" is a fascinating dramatic apprehension reinforced on several levels. Temporally, there is a comparison/contrast between the second and the nineteenth centuries, which is insisted upon in the distinction drawn between the age of Marcus Aurelius and those of Saint Louis (for the French) and of Alfred (for the English), and in the assertion that the two highly civilized centuries present their peoples with comparable trials (140). Textually, a dramatic contrast is established between Mill's *On Liberty* and Marcus Aurelius' *Meditations*, drawing into consideration the genre of moralist analysis and guidance, of which *On Liberty* is implicitly a part, as is the *Meditations*. At the center of the measuring that takes place between these two books is the peculiar character and strength of Christianity's contributions to this moralist tradition as represented by the Old and New Testaments and the *Imitation*. As they are the best of the Christian tradition, so Mill is the best of the modern non-Christian moralists (136) and Marcus Aurelius the best of the ancient non-Christian moralists, better, specifically, than Seneca, for the Romans, and Epictetus, for the Greeks (149). As the second century represents a highly civilized period when Christianity, the religion of the future, had not been quite established, so the nineteenth century represents a highly civilized period when Christianity, for many the religion of the past, has not been quite disestablished. As *dramatis personae*, Marcus Aurelius is a child of paganism who is seen as having an almost overwhelming "affinity for Christianity" (156), unconsciously "stretching out his arms for something beyond" paganism (157), while John Stuart Mill is a child of modernism who has turned his back on Christianity, seeing Christian morality as " 'falling far below the best morality of the ancients' " (133).

The dramatic irony of the central revelation of the piece is that, despite his rationalism, his style, his place at the apex of modern civilization, John Stuart Mill is inferior as a moralist to Marcus Aurelius; and Marcus Aurelius is superior as a moralist, despite his crabbed style, that of a Roman writing Greek, and despite the ineffectualness of his public life, not because of his paganism, but because of his affinity for Christianity, even though that affinity was foiled by time, place, and position. Epictetus and Mill are better reasoners; Christ and Marcus Aurelius are better moralists, the latter to the degree that his moral writings are "suffused and softened by something of this very sentiment whence Christian morality draws its best power" (136). Therefore, though Marcus Aurelius' *Meditations* may be justly called "a short masterpiece on morals" (138), Mill's *On Liberty* may not.

Moreover, throughout the essay we are reminded of metaphysical and ethical principles in direct opposition to Utilitarianism—asceticism, altruism, the dependence of the quality of an action on the cultivation of the agent performing it. Marcus Aurelius' principle of "living according to nature" (151, 152) is different in kind from the abstract "state of Nature" of the Utilitarians. Even though Arnold faults the homocentrism of Aurelius' metaphysical concept of the universe —"*all other things have been made for the sake of rational beings*" (155)— he applauds the ethical conversion of this concept into "for a man ought to consider as an enjoyment everything which it is in his power to do according to his own nature . . ." (156).

Nature then becomes a tactile truth, not a mere integer in an abstract system.

Finally, though Marcus Aurelius lacked the joy and incomparable style of Jesus, he not only had the secret of inwardness, but he was also sincere at the most fundamental of levels. So, despite the fact that "there is something melancholy, circumscribed, and ineffectual" about him (146), he can, because of the character of his personal achievement in the face of those defects, be considered as "perhaps the most beautiful figure in history" (140). He is the sort of hero that Arnold would set against the more militant heroes of Carlyle as a reminder to "our weak and easily discouraged race [of] how high human goodness and perseverance have once been carried, and may be carried again" (140).

In "Marcus Aurelius," then, Arnold follows imaginative procedures that he had followed in his poetry. He uses a *persona* to give to the moralist issue depth in human character and experience. To the supremely rational, quietly confident voice of John Stuart Mill, he counterpoints the meditative, troubled, earnest voice of Marcus Aurelius. Between them he positions the whole Christian era and suggests implicitly that his principals can be measured by their degree of affinity for it. Through a design that is both functional and non-insistent, he enables us to participate in the "emotion and inspiration" of Marcus Aurelius' private struggle after the good life while, at an almost subliminal level, we detach without contention from the inadequate morality of the Utilitarian propagandists, the very best of whom was John Stuart Mill.

Throughout *Essays in Criticism,* there is both a textual and a subtextual awareness of the point at which poetry and prose converge. Prose is freer, but poetry, if one can maintain his originality under the pressure of its formalistic demands, is more salutary. Like Maurice de Guérin, Arnold was an "ardent seeker for that mode of expression which is the most natural, happy, and true" (22). Discursive ideas may have a greater prominence in Arnold's prose than in his poetry, where thought is more fully subjected to form and form is more customarily seen as the chief device for the imaginative conversion of ideas, but they do not have the almost exclusive prominence that the commentators have given them.[17] As we know from "The Literary Influence of Academies," Arnold was far too acutely aware of the principle of literary propriety or decorum to confuse in any literal way the distinctive forms of poetry and prose. But many of the ideas of his prose are just as poetic as those of his poetry, and they come to us just as surely at the distance of form. The form is different from that of poetry at the literal, conventional level; but its function is comparable, and prose can hardly aspire to the domain of art without it.

When Arnold referred to the eighteenth century as "our great age of prose," his emphasis was as much on *great* as on *prose*. The eighteenth century's love affair with genres made it, from one point of view, the most formalistic of poetic centuries, and Arnold had no quarrel with its exquisite refinements of form. He simply saw the form (and the state of the human spirit reflected by the form) as more appropriate to the work of prose than to the work of poetry, especially an English poetry with Milton in the background and Wordsworth in the foreground. Milton himself was the greatest of a great century of prose writers (15); and while his poetry was the exemplary touchstone, in English, of the imaginative victory of style, Milton's prose was also a vehicle wholly adequate to his genius for style.

In *On Liberty,* ideas in the discursive sense are clearly predominant. The book moves by a process of mind speaking to mind through a rational network of clarification and elaboration, the appeal being essentially to the reason and the method—sometimes inductive, sometimes deductive—made up of such standard devices as analysis, definition, comparison and contrast, instances and examples for proof. *Essays in Criticism,* on the other hand, has a peculiar "mental and spiritual constitution" that far exceeds mere "intellectual definition." If its primary appeal is to intelligence, it is to an apprehension of intelligence expanded to include all aspects of a complexly cultivated consciousness—philosophical acuity, moral refinement, religious conscientiousness, aesthetic sensitivity and responsiveness—the diminishment of any part of which would significantly alter its peculiar mental and spiritual constitution.

Essays in Criticism projects a state of consciousness analogous to that which Newman describes in the Preface to the *Apologia*: "He asks what I *mean;* not about my words, not about my arguments, not about my actions, as his ultimate point, but about that living intelligence, by which I write, and argue, and act. He asks about my Mind and its Beliefs and its sentiments. . . ."[18] And we recognize this consciousness of *Essays in Criticism* by direct, internal evidence. Through its own stylistic guidance, we are instructed to give due attention and weight to its selection of its subjects or exemplary "actions"—what actually happens in the life-curves of its chief characters or *exempla*: to the effect that the architecture or design of the various essays has on the character and relevance of the book's ideas; to the role of language (diction, rhythm, image, tone) in positioning the reader in an attitudinal relationship to the importance and the accessibility of the substantive materials of the book; to the precision and adequacy of its distinctions and discriminations, whether of the outer world of sense or of the world of inner presence, of thought or of character; to the role of "emotion and inspiration" in the book's peculiar constitution and the critical effect of these on the book's intellectual fiber.

"Maurice de Guérin," the earliest of the compositions that make up *Essays in Criticism*, actually takes as its implicit but pervasive subject the poetry of prose, thus placing the issue in a key position in the growth of the volume. Though Arnold does not use a single example from Guérin's miscellaneous verses, he uses Guérin's prose remains to illustrate one of the two "grand" interpretive powers of poetry, firmly draws lines of overlap and divergence between Guérin and Keats without any need to stress the fact that the prose of the one is being compared with the poetry of the other, and ends his essay with a substantial sampling of Guérin's *The Centaur*, which he twice refers to as a "prose poem." If the reader can avoid literal-mindedness and can look at Arnold's treatment of Guérin as metaphoric and exploratory, he has both the essay as commentary (Arnold) and the essay as anthology (Guérin through Arnold) as data from which to develop a useful understanding of Arnold's sense of the qualities of poetry available to prose.

In the first place, prose that aspires to the condition of art is not philosophical or explanatory in the scientific sense, "drawing out in black and white" its message; rather, it deals with things so as "to awaken in us a wonderfully full, new, and intimate sense of them . . ." (12–13). Its primary goal is not expository or argumentative, but experiential and revelatory. For this, a writer must have "a profound and delicate sense of the life" of his subject, not simply a complete intellectual mastery of it; he must also have "an exquisite felicity in finding expressions to render that sense" (15). In other words, it is indispensable that he have an intuitive recognition that insight and language are incomplete without each other and, once fused, are inseparable dimensions of what exists. This capacity inevitably assumes both a "gifted organization" (16) and a "passion for perfection" (28). It assumes other things as well: a genuine "passion for poetry and literature" (18); an intense, unalloyed respect both for one's subject in its "smallest details" and for one's own way of seeing (visually, spiritually) that subject (20); an active, self-transformational, classical interest in the resources of one's language—its "constructions, turns of expression, delicacies of style" (21); a degree of self-awareness and a capacity for self-correction correspondent to the degree of one's faith in his own way of seeing things (22).

If one's genius is, like that of Guérin and of Keats, as an interpreter of the "natural magic" of the world, he cannot be "combative, rigid, despotic," but must be "elusive, undulating, impalpable," moved by intuition, delicate rather than energetic (23). Realization is his goal, not judgment, and his energy comes from his peculiar temperament rather than from moral or philosophical structures or enthusiasms. Even if he has a profound religious sense, which Guérin did and Keats did not, he will rebel against fixedness (17). Should there be something "morbid and excessive" in so self-consuming, so "*devouring*," a temperament (32), there may also be "something genial, outward, and sensuous," as in the case of Keats, or "something mystic, inward, and profound," as in the case of Guérin (34).

The brief anthology of Guérin's prose that the essay provides tells much the same story. Guérin's basic aesthetic authority is the authority of the eye: he sees the individually distinctive character of objects and scenes with the specificity of a Keats or a Hopkins or, among aestheticians, a Ruskin. Everything—the seer as well as the seen—is distinguished by a marked individuality. In each of his scenes drawn from nature, the principle of design is strenuously at work, so that details draw into a satisfying picture. Guérin is especially fascinated by pictures in motion, the physiognomy of nature in the process of change. His crisp pictorial images customarily have a human correspondence, the face of man seen in the face of nature, though his imaginative humanizations, being largely without philosophical content, are not subject to intellectual confusion.

In his religious meditations, he seems to be suffering from stress, as though the special effort required is contrary to his free, unthoughtful nature. But his efforts to realize in language a moment of motion in nature are suffused with sanguine, positive, joyous undertones as though something beautiful is about to yield to something yet more beautiful. And even the severely limited number of examples that Arnold gives prepares us to accept as wholly authentic in Guérin what in another might ring false: "There is one word which is the God of my imagination, the tyrant, I ought rather to say, that fascinates it, lures it onward, gives it work to do without ceasing, and will finally carry it I know not where; the word *life*" (31).

When we look at the selections from *The Centaur*, we realize immediately that, when Arnold twice called the piece a "prose poem," he was not referring to its dithyrambic qualities, its heightened rhetoric and emotional inflation, because it is entirely free of these. We see, rather, that he had in mind a marvelously delicate fictional conceit, design, and language comparable to the idylls of Theocritus. We see, too, how little the poetic qualities of the piece are obscured by its prose dress. The subject is man's relentless, perhaps obsessive, search in nature for the secrets of the universe—of origins, of destinies. The awareness inherent in the movement of the piece is that nature has never been known to give up her deepest secrets, that she has tendencies and manifestations that must be enjoyed simply in and of themselves. The imaginative fancy of a man sitting at the feet of a centaur for the wisdom of his experience is both simple and rich in metaphoric reverberations. Though the "*natural magic*" of the universe is given a metaphor through which to shine, its "*moral profundity,*" except as implicit in the conscientiousness of the human search, is quite simply foregone.

The poetic qualities that verse and prose share, then, have little to do with the mechanical characteristics of the two different conventions of writing. They are spiritual qualities of a very specific though infinitely variable kind having more to do with the peculiar "organization"—the "mental and spiritual constitution"—of the writer and his distinctive way of treating his subject than with the mechanics of either prose or verse. As, in the essay on "Heinrich Heine," Arnold quotes Goethe as having said, "the artist must work from within outwards, seeing that, make what contortions he will, he can only bring to light his own individuality" (110). As Arnold himself said in *On Translating Homer,* "Poets receive their distinctive character, not from their subject, but from their application to that subject of the ideas (to quote the *Recluse*)

> On man, on nature, and on human life,

which they have acquired for themselves."[19]

Those poetic or spiritual qualities are, then, individuality; design in both the motivational and the architectural sense; insights into one's subject that are not only original and worthy but are so deeply rooted in human nature's experience of itself that they become both a reincarnation and a reinterpretation of that experience; language that, by its selection, combination, construction, variation, both facilitates and becomes a dimension of insight. Arnold characterized poetry as "simply the most beautiful, impressive, and widely effective mode of saying things" (110), and for this both prose and verse may qualify. Of course, one who attempts to write prose that is "beautiful, impressive, and widely effective" runs the risk of being less than fully satisfying to special interest groups. Though philosophical ideas are wholly relevant to Arnold's complexly cultivated consciousness, professional philosophers will generally find his way with ideas insufficiently structured or formulaic and hence unsatisfactory. His recognition that man is essentially a moral being and his efforts to relate man's search for the good life (for happiness, symbolically speaking) to the way man thinks and feels and uses words will strike the moralist who aspires to scientific exactitude as soft and muddled. The religious fundamentalist may miss, in the book's lack of orthodoxy and of a scholastic religious vocabulary, the pervasive presence of a profound reverence for objects of spiritual longing. And the aesthetician with a strong penchant for aesthetic categories, literary definitions, and classical genres may wonder if it is literary criticism at all, in spite of the fact that the relationship between criticism and creativity is, properly perceived, its most relentless single concern.

Although, in *Essays in Criticism*, Arnold does not turn his back on these special interest groups, as he does to their equivalents in *Literature and Dogma*, they are not his particular audience. Arnold's audience in *Essays in Criticism* is that large, non-specialist group of readers who need guidance in identifying what it is they are looking for in life beyond or instead of material and sensual achievement; an audience well disposed toward objects of mental and spiritual contemplation but without a clear and adequate notion of how to approach them; persons capable of a significant degree of creative activity whose creative impulses are to some extent strangulated. They are readers for whom beauty is an authentic catalyst, who *want* to be affected, and who would like to practice trustworthy interpenetrative principles—philosophical, moral, religious, aesthetic—in their daily lives. It was to reach this audience that Arnold, without undue ostentation, brought to his prose a goodly portion of poetry—a "beautiful, impressive, and widely effective mode of saying things."

In "The Literary Influence of Academies," one of his most strategically successful essays, Arnold gets at the matter of the poetics of prose in a different way. He takes a general subject (as distinct from the life and works of a particular author), a subject that is both tricky in itself and, on the face of it, offensive to his audience, and makes an indelible impression *while proving nothing*. Hence it is one of the most challenging of his critical undertakings: (a) a matter of considerable consequence (b) directed at a potentially hostile audience (c) turning on a fundamental perception that is not susceptible of proof, (d) the very effectiveness of which depends on fine shadings and precise gradations. In the broadest terms, he builds a case for the French Academy, using such impressive authorities as Sainte-Beuve and Renan to confirm its importance and relevance to contemporary France, concedes that an English counterpart to it is neither realizable nor desirable, and then leaves his audience to mull over the implications thereof. Thus self-awareness or self-criticism is the central moral consciousness of the essay, and this implicit theme is played against the self-conceit of Lord Macaulay as measured by a moral maxim from Spinoza (232, 257).

Arnold stresses English "energy and honesty" as leading to their preeminence in poetry and science because there are, in degree, true characteristics, but also because that is the price he must pay for taking from the English "openness of mind and flexibility of intelligence," or, in the essay's own metaphors, he gives them a fine poetry in order to make it palatable to deprive them of a fine prose. He also gives the English moral conscientiousness while diminishing their intellectual conscientiousness without explicitly pointing to the fact that intellectual conscientiousness has itself an unavoidable moral side: indulgence in inadequate thoughts in impure language in a spirit of self-inflation is morally as well as intellectually indictable. But since it is suggestiveness rather than proof that he is concerned with in the essay—consciousness rather than philosophical exactitude—he makes a compromise with these issues in order to hold his audience and implant his perception. Returning to self-conceit and its baneful corollaries as both embodied by Lord Macaulay and induced in others by him, Arnold's question is not how well the English have got on without such qualities as openness of mind and flexibility of intelligence, but how well they might have got on or might get on with them.

As the examples from Newman, Jeremy Taylor, Burke, and Carlyle (245–47, including Arnold's note, 247) all show, one of

Arnold's central issues in the essay is literary *propriety* or literary *decorum*. In that context, he is following at a great and inconspicuous distance the aesthetic tradition of genre criticism which dominated the eighteenth century. Broadly conceived, poets and prose writers make different commitments to and induce different expectations in their readers, so it is aesthetically offensive when those commitments/expectations fail of fulfilment. For a serious writer to strike a false "*note*" in this matter raises the question both of his personal sincerity and of his adequacy as a guide to others, especially to young writers. If even Burke, "our greatest English prose-writer" (246), is guilty of offending the proprieties of prose without invoking the compensating proprieties of poetry, then the problem must be considered endemic to the culture, to its aesthetic expectations, and we can expect to find more flagrant examples in others. England is famous for its poets, but poets are individual growths and not transferable to the general culture—unsusceptible to imitation except, in some degree, by other poets, not by the culture as a whole. Prose, on the other hand, is transferable, and a nation that neglects its prose more directly neglects its aesthetic and its moral culture.

A more subtextual principle of "The Literary Influence of Academies" is the special turning given to the maxim "style is the man." The national self-inflation indulged in by Macaulay is echoed in the inflation of his prose style, and since that substantive self-inflation is a failure in both taste and moral refinement, so is the inflation of the prose style. It is "vulgar" and "retarding" (257) because, by virtue of Macaulay's popularity—by the degree to which he has become a sort of one-man academy of failed taste and moral impercipience—it transfers weakness, not strength, *bête*, not urbanity. Thus "style is the man" means that the quality of an individual's style cannot exceed the quality of his moral refinement: even if the *body* of one's style is impeccable, its soul will be dwarfed and shrunken unless one has conscientiously tried to put forward, not just the best one has himself thought, but the best thought available in the current of one's time. But this process of discovering the difference between the individual's own thoughts and the best thoughts of his time requires keen and honest self-awareness, for self-criticism is an indispensable aspect of criticism just as self-knowledge is the beginning of the examined life. It is at this point in the process of discovery that the moral and intellectual emerge from a common root in human nature, and the aesthetic and the moral are indissolubly connected.

Thus, in no fanciful sense, "The Literary Influence of Academies" is an essay on genres, an essay on moral-aesthetic interconnectedness, and an essay on man, demonstrating implicitly how literary criticism is integral with the oldest manifestation of literature as *a criticism of life*, namely, the classical moralist tradition. Its chief import is not that the English need to do something external, like founding an equivalent to the French Academy, but that they need to do something internal: to look at themselves honestly, admit some rather profound truths about themselves, and, by modifying both their ill-informed self-conceit and the ill-mannered results of that self-conceit, alter the very conditions, psychological and moral, that have made their worst stylistic excesses inevitable. "Know thyself" is thus put forward as a way of dissolving the false image-building of a large segment of a society for whom a writer like Macaulay is the representative spokesman.

But it is crucial, from the standpoint of criticism, to notice how broadly Arnold casts his net to catch representative spokesmen for various sections of the reading public: for the self-satisfied middle class, Macaulay; for the conservative churchman, Jeremy Taylor; for the conservative politician, Burke; for the *soi-disant* liberated intellectual, the *Saturday Review;* for the conservative moralist and man of letters, Addison; for the revolutionary aesthete, Ruskin; for the revolutionary utopianist, Carlyle; for the best-seller crowd with some moral misgivings about the Crimean involvement, Kinglake; for the poetry reader, Palgrave. And the publication of Newman's *Apologia* gives Arnold a marvelous opportunity to take advantage of the huge attention being given to the book to establish a positive touchstone of urbanity, to implant the difference between theological belief and moral refinement, and to show that what the Englishman believes about his religion is relevant to style at a deeper level than dogma.

In what sense, then, does one speak of the "poetics" of "The Literary Influence of Academies"? In the same sense that one might speak of the poetics of St. Paul's Cathedral or of Beethoven's Fifth Symphony or of the Mona Lisa: the skill with which it employs its medium; the propriety and flexibility with which it fulfills its explicit promise; the pleasing surprises with which its originality even of explicit ideas surpasses the usual expectations; the highly suggestive manner in which it reaches far beyond its explicit subject and makes of it the metaphor of a far more encompassing subject; the implicit way in which it deploys its various parts and takes hold of the reader at a subliminally affective level, manages to "do the thing shall breed the thought, / Nor wrong the thought, missing the mediate word."[20] It does not try to *be* a poem at some transparent level such as the first paragraph quoted from Ruskin (251); rather, it employs "the form, the method of evolution, the precision, the proportions, the relations of the parts to the whole" as a poet, architect, painter, or composer might employ them without any sacrifice of the piece's distinction within the proprieties of its own genre.

The precision, transparency, affectiveness of language, the indispensability of a genuinely critical, outwardly measuring self-awareness, the delicacy, justness, and radiance of insight—these are the chief *loci* of the creative consciousness of *Essays in Criticism*, and nowhere, not even in "The Function of Criticism at the Present Time," do they get richer exposure than in "Joubert." "Joubert" is one of Arnold's truly great and characteristic essays, worthy of a place at the apex of his achievement alongside such masterpieces of tact and strategy as "Wordsworth," "Byron," "The Function of Criticism at the Present Time," the Preface to the First Edition of *Poems* (1853), and "The Study of Poetry." Its title-subject is just as obscure now as he was in the early 1860s; but the critical ore that Arnold drew from that obscurity is still "beautiful, impressive, and widely effective" to those who really get to know it. Joubert is admittedly a minor genius, but Arnold seems to have less reason to quarrel with him than with others of more general fame, including Spinoza, Heine, and Marcus Aurelius. He has not shaped the future, and he directed none of his energy toward that goal. But in his person and in his time, he is the "ideal" of *Essays in Criticism*, the surrogate *us*, so to speak, if we end "by [fully] receiving its influence, and by undergoing its law" (106).

In the distant background seems to be the figure of Pascal. Although Joubert in no sense challenges Pascal, he belongs to the legitimate line of Pascal's descendants. Joubert is the author of *pensées, sententiae, maxims* in the classical French tradition; and since he was more ambitious of self-development ("perfection") than of literary fame, it is natural to think of his formulations as essentially self-instructive, like those of Marcus Aurelius. But besides being a "religious philosopher" rather than a moralist, Joubert was very much concerned with the physiognomy of style and with an unattainable ideal of language. Joubert's maxims constitute an extraordinary example of literary conscientiousness that does not have an equal even in Coleridge: criticism that has a high proportion of self-criticism coupled with so intense a regard for language that Joubert strives, even for his own edification, his own delicate respect for the truth, to say things perfectly because until they are perfectly said, they cannot be perfectly true.

Thus, after a general introduction, Arnold compares/contrasts Joubert with Coleridge in such a way as both to distinguish between their respective strengths and to position Joubert as really the more accessible and serviceable of the two. Coleridge is a founder in English, as Joubert is not in France, a fact which magnifies Coleridge's importance in his native land and in his native tongue; he was needed more in England than Joubert was needed in France. But setting that aside, Arnold's brief anthology of Joubert's maxims—on language, literature, the Bible and religion, politics—effectively establishes for Joubert a credibility *in English* that, for the general cultivated reader, Coleridge does not have even *in English*, while Coleridge has little or no credibility in France at all.

Arnold first gives careful critical attention to Joubert's perfectionism with respect to language (194–97); and while, as a practical critic, Arnold clearly feels that Joubert has pressed this matter beyond the limits of the practically useful ("something a little too ethereal," 196), he yet recognizes it as the admirable magnification of an essentially French trait which has great value as an ideal, clearly seeing Joubert's devotion to language as a chief source of the "delicacy and penetration" (198) of his thoughts and maxims. But though his attentiveness to language is indispensable to Joubert's perceptual achievements, those achievements go far beyond language and are conspicuously successful wherever his attention turns. As Coleridge is not to be trusted on matters French, so Joubert is not to be trusted on matters English (on Milton, for example); however, on matters French, he is impeccable. And this is the underlying strategy of Arnold's essay. Working on the assumption that "as to the [positive] estimate of its own authors every nation is the best judge" (190), he uses Joubert as a way of getting inside the French critical psyche in order to give the English reader the best possible French evaluation of French cultural and literary figures and movements.

The establishment of Joubert's authority despite his anonymity and the gradual build-up of his opinions on matters having general currency with the cultivated English reader determines the structure of the essay: his role at the University; the high regard in which he was held among savants; his similarities to Coleridge; his thoughts on language, the diplomacy of religion, the different appeals of Catholicism and Protestantism, the Old Testament and the New, the Jansenists and the Jesuits, Romantic Modernist fiction, Plato, Nicole, Bossuet, Racine, Boileau. These are all useful and primary topics in and of themselves, but they climax in Joubert's critical judgments of Voltaire and Rousseau and his discriminations between them. They are the most imposing French cult figures of modern times, having large currency and little just critical evaluation in contemporary England (205–06), and they are the figures to whom the young writer might most naturally look for guidance. Joubert's comments on them illustrate "the soundness and completeness of his judgments" (205), while at the same time they implant a serious caution to unwary young writers tempted to emulate them. Joubert's comments on political matters—the comments of one who lived through the French Revolution (he would have been thirty-nine during the Reign of Terror)—have about them a restraint, a historical rootedness, and a philosophical sagacity in sharp contrast to the furious excursions of Carlyle. Finally, Arnold uses Joubert—now established for the English reader in considerable depth—as a positive model against which to measure not only a notorious contemporary of Coleridge's, Lord Jeffrey, but also a notorious contemporary of his own, Lord Macaulay, in order to reveal how essentially vulgar these notorious Englishmen of succeeding generations really are.

Thus "Joubert" is an extraordinarily strategic essay, its effectiveness working at a subliminal level and the *shape* of the essay propelling its message as forcefully as its assertions. And it beautifully answers its initiating question—"Why should we ever treat of any dead authors but the famous ones?" (183)—by showing clearly that considerable value lies in the imaginative way in which the subject is apprehended and treated as well as in the subject itself.

In "Spinoza and the Bible," Arnold treats, not a "religious philosopher"of a general humanistic sort like Joubert or, ideally, ourselves, but one of the supreme religious and moral philosophers of modern times. In Spinoza, a Jew, he finds an equivalent exemplification of his principle that one's own countrymen are the best judges of the meaning and significance of one's literary work. For general sanity and an impeccable methodology (the use of evidence, the placing of language in its proper, preeminent position, the making of connections that are wholly reasonable and stunningly imaginative, the drawing of necessary distinctions, the pushing of individuated concepts to their truly meaningful conclusions) this mid-seventeenth-century document of Spinoza's, *Tractatus Theologico-Politicus*, is not improved upon even by the very best Biblical criticism of the nineteenth century, and is vastly superior to most of it. Moreover, Arnold's précis of the book (160–69) is a unique sequence in *Essays in Criticism*—its only severe philosophical exemplum—and represents a rhetorical change of pace that shows both how the literary critic differs from the philosopher in subject matter and style and how, for a brief, concentrated period, the critic may make philosophy central to his more eclectic purposes.

Arnold's estimate of the then rather obscure Spinoza is startlingly high: he calls him "the central point of interest" in the "history of modern philosophy" (159); he pairs him with Plato in order of importance (181); he has Heine deflate Hegel in Spinoza's favor (182); he measures Voltaire and David Friedrich Strauss down by comparison with him (179); he makes him the fountainhead for Lessing, Goethe, and Heine. Arnold is thereby able to perform a function that the literary critic must, in degree, share with the great philosopher, that is, to edify, and Arnold's "Spinoza and the Bible" becomes an edifying, a clarifying, and a reconciling fable for "the Present Time." Through his exemplification of how Spinoza put the Bible on new and sound foundations and yet increased rather than decreased his devotion to "love of God" as the "*summum bonum*," he implicitly contradicts the wave of negative and inadequate criticism of the Bible in the nineteenth century.

Spinoza is to the Synagogue that anathematized him in 1656 what Newman is to the synod of Anglican bishops that condemned him in 1841—the great betrayer. But to the modern world, he is the great guide and consoler. By making necessary distinctions between faith and natural history, between theology and morality, between epistemology and ethics, he established bases for an honorable truce in the war between science and theology, and in his personal example, he confirmed that faith and reason could meet and reinforce human life in the most respectable and substantive fashion. Spinoza's book is not, in all its parts, satisfying, nor are Newman's writings. Both Spinoza and Newman appear in certain respects to be "*in the air*" (174), though Arnold's unease with Spinoza at least is not with specific contradictions so much as with a lack of explicit clarification on certain fundamental issues on Spinoza's part (e.g., miracles). Newman's public orthodoxy on the matter of Revelation, he saw, however, as an anachronism, a position taken and clung to in contradiction to the imperatives of the modern *Zeitgeist*.[21] But Newman and Spinoza are alike not only in making essential, finely discriminated distinctions (reason vs. faith, epistemology vs. ethics, essentials vs. accidents) but also in making the love of God the supreme goal of even the most intellectually refined of human spirits.

On the more speculative side, it is on the basis of two fundamental principles that Spinoza laid his hand upon the future—upon Lessing, Goethe, and Heine: (1) his denial of final causes, putting man within the frame of the total universe, not seeing the universe designed to the exclusive interests of man, and (2) his active, joyous stoicism. In the one, he clarifies the human situation; in the other, he consoles man, makes him accepting of the new order of truth. In the first, he is at odds with the spirit of the Old Testament, in the second, with the spirit of the New; but in both he is the voice of the future. In the one, he enunciates what Lessing called the only possible "view of life" (182); through the latter, he avoids the spirit of demolition central to the criticism of Voltaire and Strauss, and, through a combination of the two, he escapes the global irreligion of Hegel. Thus Spinoza, in the image of the ideal philosopher, represents *par excellence* the ideal of the "intellectual life" (178): he released certain governing ideas into the general consciousness (175); he made clear the relevance of those ideas to the basic life of man in this world (175); and he did this in an edifying fashion, through a spirit of constructive, of consoling, reconciliation with a new view of life.

The literary critic, by bringing Spinoza forward in this fashion, provides his own readers, who are much more numerous than the readers of Spinoza himself, with indispensable guidance in dealing with the multitude of modern philosophers. He not only analyzes, he converts. And though Spinoza is never shifted from the central concern of the critic's treatment, the critic's own contribution, though clearly secondary, is, from the point of view of most of his readers, crucial. Indeed, the proper relation of the critic both to his subject and to his reader is one of the central constructions of *Essays in Criticism*.

"Heinrich Heine" is the essay in which Arnold takes his leap into the literature of social conscience, into literature's sense of the modern spirit and its role as liberator of the soul of man. At the heart of the essay is the distinction between the conventional wisdom, on the one hand, and, on the other, the forward-moving *Zeitgeist* that makes the conventional wisdom a bastion of the outmoded at the very moment it becomes strong and comfortable. Arnold's sense of epoch—what is needed, how literature succeeds or fails in delivering what is needed—has, thus, a particular cultural manifestation to work on, to measure. Goethe is the great foundation figure; Byron and Shelley are the high-minded but incompetent misfirers; Carlyle, through an infection of international provincialism that crippled his genius, is the great but failed physician, diagnosing inaccurately the sickness of the age, the victim to a degree of a misconceived, though glamorous, Romantic Medievalism; Wordsworth, Scott, and Keats, though they fail less spectacularly, more or less do fail. The lesson for literary criticism is a fundamental one: without this keen and firm sense of epoch, the critic could not justly place Heine, would have inadequate data for measuring him, could even take him at his own word and still not genuinely understand what that word meant.

The composition of this essay, then, becomes a self-processing of inestimable value to Arnold as it looks forward boldly if unconsciously to *Culture and Anarchy:* the modern spirit, the heavy weight of Philistinism, the true reality of Hebraism and Hellenism, the qualitative distinction between a culture drenched in ideas (Germany), a culture peculiarly practiced in the application of ideas to life (France), and a culture, in this case non-national, that conscientiously desires that the idea monitor the culture (the Jew). Here also we have a revelation that, while it may seem obvious, is little noticed—namely, that there is hardly any point in fretting over the question of the absolute truth of Arnold's characterizations of the German, the Frenchman, the Jew, and the Greek when what is important is their approximate, essentially literary, truth. They give body to metaphoric ways of perceiving; they are verbal insights, not scientific, "ethnological" facts. There is enough *prima facie* truth in them to make them meaningful and to enable them to function as concepts. Whether or not they have more truth than that is debatable, but that they have more is not essential. They are models of the making of cultural metaphors which, in a more highly developed state, will make *Culture and Anarchy* an original and startling essay on man. Arnold's metaphors do not need to be literally, scientifically true to be extraordinarily effective: that is their distinction as "literary art."

Crucial to Arnold's leap into social consciousness in "Heinrich Heine" is the need still to keep literary criticism literary, to keep it from getting lost in general cultural, historical commentary. He points to this need explicitly by his stress on "ascertain[ing] the master-current in the *literature* of an epoch and distinguish[ing] it from all minor currents . . . " (107, emphasis added) and implicitly by the care with which he *generalizes about the age from the literature rather than about the literature from the age*. Thus his citing of Heine's phrase about Goethe—a writer "should control his subject-matter and keep himself beautifully objective, as the artistic school would have it, and as Goethe has done" (109), that is, be "*hübsch objectiv*" (125)—has fundamental relevance to Arnold's own critical-cultural method and is one of the sources of his peculiar strength in converting literary criticism from a narrow interest in *belles-lettres* to concern for the controlling spiritual characteristics of an epoch or age. What Arnold essentially does is extend to a third correlational analogy Goethe's analysis of an artist's relationship to his era:

> "Through me the German poets have become aware that, as man must live from within outwards, so the artist must work from within outwards, seeing that, make what contortions he will, he can only bring to light his own individuality. I can clearly mark where this influence of mine has been felt; there arises out of it a kind of poetry of nature, and only in this way is it possible to be original."

As the artist must work from within outward in the creation of a significant work of art, so the critic must work from within the work of art outward in order to penetrate this "poetry of nature," to see what inner conditions the tendencies of an age have been subjected to, and thereby to understand what is essential rather than minor or tangential about the age which, through art, he is trying to comprehend. So Goethe becomes the foundation figure of modernism, not only through the outward sagacity with which he read it, but also through the inner sagacity with which he guided artists to the right way of dealing with it—from inside out and with a "*hübsch objectiv*" detachment that could enable them to be both idiosyncratic and superbly relevant rather than the victims of the age's "multitudinousness." Involvement in political practice is a contradiction to this (118); yielding to such fascinating but partial solutions as that embodied in Medievalism (119) is a contradiction to it. The grand but ultimately inadequate apprehensions of "stock romanticism" and "stock classicism" (122) foreshorten its relevance, as do the sometimes admirable but inevitably faulted revolts against the conventional wisdom of a single nation (120), even of a Germany, even of a France. It is not enough to be a man of genius, like Carlyle. One must touch, besides the great points of a single nation, "all the great points in the career of the human race" (119) and subject *them* to the metamorphosis of one's own personal individuality.

Recognition that other essays in Arnold's classic volume are worthy competitors for our critical applause does not, of course, diminish our admiration for "The Function of Criticism at the Present Time." It is one of the most accomplished, most masterful essays of its kind in English, and none of those who have since used it as a point of departure and challenge—Eliot, Leavis, Bateson, Frye—has ever bettered it. It is not a manifesto in the oratorical modern sense; and even as a polemic, it is reasoned and restrained in the finest classical tradition. It is not only the most adequate, accessible, and creative handling of a critical idea, but it is also the most poetic. It is a conversion into subject, structure, and language of the *meaning* of Matthew Arnold, of his "living intelligence," his "Mind and its Beliefs and its sentiments."[22]

Its argument is an *action*, a movement of mind and spirit along a narrative curve that begins with a question or dilemma: is criticism really such a "low" and "inglorious employment" as Wordsworth said it was? (259); and it ends with a resolution or revelation: that criticism, so long as it is genuine, can give us a "joyful sense of creativity," can be for us "the great proof of being alive" (285). This might seem to be a rather fanciful turning to what, in its rawest initial form, is a debater's question unless we remember that the truly operative concern of the essay is "function" (action), that the notion of function is being measured within the manifestations of a particular but metaphoric time-frame ("at the Present Time," in the current phase of the *Zeitgeist*), and that the general field of the essayist's consciousness is human nature itself (e.g., "poor human nature," 259, 272; "weak humanity," 272; "men," "a man," *passim*). Therefore, though the essay follows a wholly legitimate intellectual line of development, the indispensability of a great age of widely current ideas to a great age of literary creativity, it draws deeper, more personally experiential waters as it develops its universally human insight that "the highest function of man," "the true happiness of all men," is "a free creative activity." It is this "free creative activity" which must be exercised by the overwhelming majority of men "in other ways than in producing great works of literature and art . . . " (260).

In pursuit of this more enveloping insight, "The Function of Criticism at the Present Time" is enlarged, through a gradual metamorphosis of its subject, to encompass, besides an essay on literary criticism, an essay on man. An intellectual argument is transformed into a moral action, and the refined activity of the happy few is expanded to include the quality of life of Everyman. Moreover, the processing of the subject of the essay inheres in the essay's manner: the author-narrator actually takes the reader "well disposed toward objects of mental and spiritual contemplation but without a clear and adequate notion of how to approach them" on a thinking tour of some representative metaphors or reference points of his intellectual life—the Romantic movement, the French Revolution, eminent organs of the fourth estate (the *Edinburgh Review*, the *Quarterly Review*, the *British Quarterly Review*, the *Times*), the expostulations of such dithyrambic extollers of " 'our unrivalled happiness' " as Sir Charles Adderley and Mr. Roebuck, the daily press, the British Constitution, the legions of Liberals, Biblical criticism, the architecture of public institutions, the Divorce Court. By providing an exemplary running commentary on these widely varied but representative objects of intellectual interest and engagement, Arnold clarifies and implants a corresponding variety of critical principles and affirmative processes.

The critical principles, as they emerge organically from the movement of the text, are clear and crisp. *The meaning of criticism* is *"a disinterested endeavour to learn and propagate the best that is known and thought in the world" (283). The object of criticism* is, "in all branches of knowledge . . . to see the object as in itself it really is" (258, 261). *The motive of criticism* is two-fold—self-renewal and the renewal of one's culture (260). *The nourisher of criticism* is fresh and adequate knowledge (262, 283), the communication of which is *criticism's chief goal,* while the critic's judgment is *a secondary goal,* "a sort of companion and clue" to fresh knowledge (283). *The corrective or stabilizer of criticism* is, on the one hand, the capacity to return upon oneself and, like Burke, to see the merits of a case differently from the way one had previously seen them (267) and, on the other, the avoidance of abstractions and the maintenance of a "lively consciousness of the truth of what one is saying" (283), of a sort of tactility between the object and one's comments on the object. *The subtlest eroders of criticism* are a well-intentioned but misguided eagerness to put criticism, once some degree of critical perspective has been achieved, to practical uses *(passim)* and, a corollary to this, an inadequate faith that, in the long run, criticism which will be most serviceable is that which is most deeply engaged with truth and most completely detached from programmatic implementation (269, 275).

The affirmative processes which the essay implants function, in the term of the title, at a more implicit, subliminal, subconsciously organic level. Because readers' responses to these affirmative processes are subjective, they will vary according to their individual sympathy with what the author is attempting to do and their capacity to undergo its influence, but the very fame of the essay suggests that, for most readers, it is in fact profoundly affective. Just what those affirmative processes have been, just what the essay has *done* to the reader, is celebrated and reinforced in the language, tone, and substance—in the "emotion and inspiration," *l'effusion et l'onction*, the poetry—of the final paragraphs.

The reader is thereby brought to a restrained but nonetheless intense recognition, perhaps even a resolution, that he should know more, especially more about the "intellectual and spiritual" perceptions and aspirations of peoples other than his own, that he would in fact like to qualify for membership in this great European federation. He, too, would like to be a man of "insight and conscience" rather than "a poor, starved, fragmentary, inadequate" creature. Since he is entirely capable of being "sincere, simple, flexible, ardent, ever widening [his] knowledge," this critical process is, in very truth and *for him*, an open road to creativity and to the "great happiness and the great proof of being alive" that creativity offers. Although he will never be an Æschylus or a Shakespeare, he can travel the road that leads toward them, and may, by the way he conducts his life *at the present time*, make it easier for some other person to be an Æschylus or a Shakespeare *at some future time*. The argument of the essay has certainly contributed to this result, but the action, as in a poem, has brought it about and determined the literary decorum with which it is handled, rich in poetic energy, but not a prose poem.

Arnold (or, since the author sees himself in a certain metaphoric way having a poetic design upon a certain metaphoric type of reader, the speaker of the essay) characterizes the "idea" in which *Essays in Criticism* had its "origin" and has its "unity" as follows: "There is so much inviting us!—what are we to take? what will nourish us in growth toward perfection?" (284). It is the most encompassing, while the most wholly secular, of spiritual questions, including in its frame our minds, our hearts, our consciences, both our reverence for beauty and truth and our sense of a personal moral responsibility toward them. It is the "*note*" which is struck again and again throughout the essays generally and throughout "The Function of Criticism at the Present Time" in particular. The quest for perfection is refracted through many tropes—*adequacy, art, criticism, culture, disinterestedness, distinction, edification, epochs, genius, happiness, history, human nature, ideas, imagination, intelligence, knowledge, language, liberty, light, literature, modernity, morality, the national character, nature, paganism, Philistinism, poetry, practice, prophecy, race, reality, reason, religion, revelation, romanticism, science, society, the spirit, style, truth, the world*—and the reader of Arnold's critical prose gradually comes to recognize that Arnold has infused each of them with his distinctive spiritual presence. However, the "idea" which they illuminate ultimately is the idea of perfection. These tropes insensibly penetrate the psyche of the reader, recondition it, return its hardness to solution, impregnate its prose with poetry, and direct his mind while capturing, to a palpable degree, his will.

Arnold's prose is rich in individual poetic effects, such as the bold, precarious, repetitive counterpointing of the relentlessly severe phrase "*Wragg is in custody*" to the self-blinding self-conceit of Adderley's and Roebuck's dithyrambs or "defiant songs of triumph" (271–74) and the many constructions, turns of expression, delicacies of style which have a mnemonic value that catches the ear and lingers there. But, however much one may relish these particular surfacings of Arnold's instinct for poetry, one may see Arnold's fundamental poetics working at a deeper, steadier level: in his statement through design, the grace, precision, vigor, and variety of his language and language rhythms, the imaginative habit of mind that invests even the most expository examples with metaphoric significance, the marvelously organic way in which Arnold gradually transforms a specific issue from a topical reference point to a frame of reference as large as one dimension of life itself and converts a reader from the role of intellectual onlooker to a fully immersed participant in the drama of consciousness, the act of enlargement, inherent in the very movement of an essay or collection of essays. These are the profoundly imaginative characteristics of Arnold's prose, and their persistent presence in his critical writings enables them to meet even the chief *poetic* rubrics of his age—his own characterization of poetry as "*a criticism of life*" (209); and Browning's "Art may tell a truth / Obliquely, do the thing shall breed the thought, / Nor wrong the thought, missing the mediate word";[23] and Tennyson's "Poetry is like shot-silk with many glancing colours."[24]

NOTES

1. Eleven volumes (Ann Arbor: University of Michigan Press, 1960–77). All references to Arnold's prose except the letters are to this edition, page references being given in parentheses in the text.
2. *Matthew Arnold* (New York: Macmillan, 1902), p. 74.
3. Since there is no ambiguity as to what text is being spoken of, the title of the book will be simplified in the remainder of this article to *Essays in Criticism.*
4. They are printed in *The Complete Prose Works* in the order of their original publication except that the date of composition, when it makes a difference, is given priority over the date of publication. Arnold had added "A Persian Passion Play," which is held over to Volume VII, in 1875 to justify a higher price for the volume. See William E. Buckler, *Matthew Arnold's Books: Toward a Publishing Diary* (Geneva and Paris: E. Droz, 1958), pp. 72–73.
5. See Lionel Trilling, *Matthew Arnold* (New York: W. W. Norton, 1939), and, for Eliot, the prose works from *The Sacred Wood* (1920) forward.
6. I include in this evaluation the work of H. W. Garrod, *Poetry and the Criticism of Life* (Cambridge, Mass.: Harvard University Press, 1931) and F. R. Leavis, "Arnold as Critic," *Scrutiny,* VII (Dec. 1938), 319–332.
7. Frederic E. Faverty, *Matthew Arnold, the Ethnologist* (Evanston: Northwestern University Press, 1951); William Robbins, *The Ethical Idealism of Matthew Arnold* (Toronto: University of Toronto Press, 1959); M. Sells, *Matthew Arnold and France: the Poet* (Cambridge: Cambridge University Press, 1961, rev. ed. 1970).
8. E. K. Brown, *Matthew Arnold: a Study in Conflict* (Chicago: University of Chicago Press, 1948).
9. D. G. James, *Matthew Arnold and the Decline of English Romanticism* (Oxford: Oxford University Press, 1961).
10. Geoffrey Tillotson, for example, in "Arnold and Pater: Critics Historical, Aesthetic and Unlabelled," in *Criticism and the Nineteenth Century* (London: Athlone Press, 1951), and "Matthew Arnold's Prose: Theory and Practice," in *The Art of Victorian Prose,* edd. George Levine and William Madden (New York: Oxford University Press, 1968).
11. William A. Madden, *Matthew Arnold: A Study of the Aesthetic Temperament in Victorian England* (Bloomington: Indiana University Press, 1967).
12. For example, William Robbins, in *The Arnoldian Principle of Flexibility,* English Literary Studies, University of Victoria, 1979, and Park Honan, *The Arnoldian,* 8 (Fall, 1980).
13. In "The Function of Criticism at the Present Time," for example, Arnold uses Goethe repeatedly as his touchstone for modern sagacity; but in the textual background are the unnamed but persistent figures of Plato and

Aristotle, the one as the classical spokesman for the "right tone and temper of mind," the other as the source of the fundamental idea that each thing (here criticism) should fufil the law of its own being (e.g., p. 282).

14. *Complete Prose Works*, VI, 265.
15. *Letters of Matthew Arnold, 1848–1888*, ed. G. W. E. Russell (London: Macmillan, 1895), I, 287.
16. Mill's characterization of Christian morality, as quoted by Arnold (133).
17. Little or no attention has been given to the poetics of Arnold's prose, previous emphasis having been on his ideas, his argumentative techniques, and his style. John Holloway's chapter on Arnold in *The Victorian Sage* (London: Macmillan, 1953) is a sensitive, constructive study of his argumentative method, its application to *Essays in Criticism* being worked out in *The Charted Mirror* (London: Routlege and Paul, 1960); Geoffrey Tillotson's essay on "Matthew Arnold's Prose: Theory and Practice" (*The Art of Victorian Prose*, edd. Levine and Madden) stays distressingly close to syntax, wording, and levels of usage; and Robert A. Donovan's "The Method of Arnold's *Essays in Criticism*" (*PMLA*, LXXI [Dec. 1956], 922–31) concentrates, in a very general way, on four elements—the French influence, the theme of Philistinism, the comparative critical method, and the aim "to inculcate intelligence"—which are quite external to the concerns of the present essay.
18. *Newman: Prose and Poetry*, ed. Geoffrey Tillotson (Cambridge, Mass.: Harvard University Press, 1970), p. 577.
19. *Complete Prose Works*, I, 210.
20. Robert Browning, *The Ring and the Book*, ed. F. G. Kenyon (London: Smith Elder, 1912), XII, 860–61.
21. *Literature and Dogma, Complete Prose Works*, VI, 377.
22. See note 18, above.
23. See note 20, above.
24. As quoted in *The Poems of Tennyson*, ed. Christopher Ricks (London: Longman, 1969), p. 1463.

Facing the Enemy Within

An Examination of the Moralist Mythos in *Culture and Anarchy*

In the "Introduction" to *Culture and Anarchy*,[1] Matthew Arnold said that, in his opinion, "the speech most proper, at present, for a man of culture to make to a body of his fellow-countrymen . . . is Socrates': *Know thyself!*" He thus rooted his *Essay in Political and Social Criticism*, an essay which wears contemporaneousness like an identifying badge and takes on a generation of Liberal social and political advocates in direct, toe-to-toe fashion, quite unmistakably in the classical moralist tradition. Adopting his motto from Jesus, his theme from the temple of Apollo at Delphi, and his imaginative literary guidance from Socrates, he entered the lists of modern controversy agile, supremely armed, and, by the test of normal expectation, subtly disguised. In one sense, the disguise was engagingly transparent. Persons sophisticated enough to be regular readers of such magazines as the *Cornhill* and the *Pall Mall Gazette*[2] and to have an interest in the internal sparrings of the periodical press would expect a practicing poet[3] of a conspicuously classical bent and a Professor of Poetry at Oxford to travel a high moralist road. Many of them would remember that, by Newman's account in *The Scope and Nature of University Education*, Oriel College, where, according to the title-page, Arnold was formerly a Fellow, had been the foundation from which the great apology for classical humanism had emanated a generation or so earlier. But though poets, professors of poetry, and Oriel fellows could be expected to take such edifying moralist positions quite regularly, indeed quite properly, they could hardly expect to be taken seriously, especially by the power brokers of their generation. Indeed, the very light-heartedness of his way of proceeding, his turn for wit, gaiety, and the most scintillating irony, sufficiently proved that Matthew Arnold was no exception. It was delicious to see certain over-solemn, over-confident, over-eager public figures discomfited by a sprightly academic, but his role as gadfly was too deftly played to betoken any more fundamental purpose than that.

Even the widow of Thomas Arnold was troubled by his manner. The style was too flippant and the ostensible purpose too frivolous, and it not only made the son vulnerable to demeaning journalistic attacks but also inevitably invited odious and perhaps telling comparisons between him and his late father.[4] Arnold tried repeatedly to reassure her that he knew exactly what he was doing as to both style and purpose. When he heard from his sister Jane that Mrs. Arnold did "not quite like" "My Countrymen" (*Cornhill*, February 1866), he told her that he was

> sure it was wanted, and will do good; and this . . . I really wish to do, and have my own ideas as to the best way of doing it. . . . there are certain things which it needs great dexterity to say in a receivable manner at all; and what I had to say, I could only get said, to my thinking, in the manner I have said it.[5]

His ironic letters continued to appear in the *Pall Mall Gazette*, and on July 27, 1866, he again expressed faith in the technique he had adopted:

> I understand what you feel about my graver and gayer manner, but there is a necessity in these things, and one cannot always work precisely as one would. To be able to work anyhow for what one wishes—*always supposing one has real faith that what one wishes is good and needful*—is a blessing to be thankfully accepted.[6]

After the articles that make up *Culture and Anarchy* had begun to appear, he wrote to her (December 5, 1867):

> For my part, I see more and more what an effective weapon, in a confused, loud-talking, clap-trappy country like this, where every writer and speaker to the public tends to say rather more than he means, is *irony*, or according to the strict meaning of the original Greek word, the saying rather less than one means. The main effect I have had on the mass of noisy claptrap and inert prejudice which chokes us has been, I can see, by the use of this weapon; and now, when people's

> minds are getting widely disturbed and they are beginning to ask themselves whether they have not a great deal that is new to learn, to increase this feeling in them is more useful than ever.[7]

The rather more that he meant than he was saying in *Culture and Anarchy* had been expressed some two years earlier: "I, who do not believe that the essential now to be done is to be done through this external machinery of Reform bills and extension of the franchise, yet look upon the outward movement as a necessary part of the far more vital inward one, and think it important accordingly."[8]

He was delighted with the way his chief terms in *Culture and Anarchy* gained general currency because of his faith in their penetrating *symbolic* working: "The merit of terms of this sort ["sweetness and light," "Philistinism," "Hebraism and Hellenism"] is that they fix in people's minds the *things* to which they refer."[9] He also expressed a profound faith in the *symbolic truth* of the chapters later entitled "Hebraism and Hellenism" and "*Porro Unum Est Necessarium*": "The chapters on Hellenism and Hebraism are in the main, I am convinced, so true that they will form a kind of centre for English thought and speculation on the matters treated in them."[10] "Hebraism" and "Hellenism" are not scientific or philosophical terms, certainly. The historical framework that Arnold supplies for them in Chapter IV is clearly fictional—an aid to reflection rather than to autonomous fact. They are symbolic instruments of release from an infinity of factual details, metaphors of consciousness by which one can achieve a satisfying, almost tactile sense of the fluid movements of time and of the relationship to the master-currents within the self of an image of history that is both essentially spiritual and imaginatively contemporaneous. They create a context of reciprocation between the self and the not-self, the *now* and the *then*, and supply an externalizing structure for the study of oneself, a way of avoiding the demon of self-consciousness that had made the pursuit of the Apollonian principle so harrowing an experience to the "sons" of the Romantics.[11]

One begins to suspect, then, that Arnold has assumed the moralist's role in *Culture and Anarchy* in a far deeper sense than is usually thought, which explains the inner, dramatic truth of the book to which everything else is a genuine rather than a transparent disguise. So deep was his commitment that he could hold steady even in the face of his mother's discomfort with the appearance of mere "persiflage" because he knew how deep, true, and needful was the book's innermost flow. He believed, as Tennyson had believed in casting *The Princess*, that he could not hope to get a hearing for his profounder purpose unless he came at it obliquely, appearing to do one thing while he was intensely, if feignedly, engaged in doing quite another. The marvelous nimbleness of the book is, in effect, an expression—a literarily successful expression—of the hyper-perceptive state necessary to succeed at his imaginatively evasive ends, so that the book's inner dramatic truth is being pursued, not in the vague, descriptive sense of general intention and import, but in the particular, functional sense of design and maneuver having a working analogy in religious discipline, spiritual exercises, and the subtle, wholly circumspect relentlessness of a Socratic dialogue. In short, "*Know thyself*" is indeed the fundamental and controlling concern of *Culture and Anarchy*, informing its mythos, shaping its architecture, monitoring its metaphors, and illustrating how a modern poet (Arnold) succeeds at an imaginatively organic transformation of an ancient literary model (Plato).

Even though, like Tennyson in the early stages of composing *In Memoriam* and *Idylls of the King*, Arnold did not have in his conscious mind a fully designed *Culture and Anarchy* when he delivered "Culture and Its Enemies" as his final lecture as Professor of Poetry at Oxford in June 1867 and published it in the July number of the *Cornhill*, it is all there: the subject or action or myth and the implicit imperatives by which the ultimate design is inherent in and under the control of the action or myth. Present are not only the predominant metaphors—the narrative voice or *persona*, the antiphonal styles, the insistent contemporaneousness, the mediating presence of Jesus and Socrates in the background—but also the enlarging analogies (poetry, religion, philosophy) and the deeply imbedded key for their converion into a truly functional, wholly operative relevance (that endlessly rewarding critical process set in motion by "reading, observing, thinking" in an attentive and dispassionate manner of which *Culture and Anarchy* is itself a self-fulfilling model, as are the examples of Jesus in the New Testament and of Socrates in the Platonic dialogues). By the very act of coming to full terms with the "Introduction" and "Sweetness and Light," which "Culture and Its Enemies" ultimately became in *Culture and Anarchy,* we know that the central figure of "machinery" is cunningly self-reflexive.

The almost universal tendency to read life mechanically, to confuse the means with the end, applies to the way we habitually *read books*, including this book, and the way we *see* and *think about* life generally. The narrative *persona's* talk about the fetish that the nation has made of freedom, population, coal, railroads, wealth, and religion is, if looked at "attentively and dispassionately" (95), really talk about us: our share in ordinary human nature's self-indulgent neglect of order or distrust of and restless response to authority *(freedom)* and in ordinary human nature's ingrained tendency to nest and propagate *(population)*, to get and be comfortable *(coal)*, to prize physical convenience *(railroads)*, to put a very high premium on material security *(wealth)*, and to wrap ourselves in a mechanical cloak of righteousness *(religion)*. Though the language and sentiments have, on the one hand, a highly familiar ring through their association with the pulpit or the lectern, the Bible or the school classics, they gradually begin to work in a more immediate, less institutionalized way, getting closer to where we actually live and assuming a new and altogether more interesting aspect. Evolutionary in this context, culture is in truth a total state of human *being* that stirs into life some dwarfed, inner, almost alien dimension of ourselves, and enables us to see our own faces in the mirrors of Mr. Bright and Mr. Harrison, recognizing that the enemies of culture are in our everyday, thoroughly human, quite ordinary selves.

Thus the reciprocation between culture and religion has already begun. "*The kingdom of heaven is within you*" (94) is, at a threshold level, being converted from a dictum to a dramatically or processively verified personal experience. Reflecting this movement, the book's range—the parameters of appropriateness which will determine the decorum of its literary procedures, its tone, the field of its action and argument, the character of its metaphors, the posture of its narrative *persona*—is being firmly established. The dualism which it creates in a very delicate, tentative, and fluid way is nothing so lurid, substantively, as a fire-and-brimstone Manichaeism and nothing so rigid and methodologically systematic as a Hegelian dialectic.[12] The counterpoint to "*The kingdom of heaven is within you*" is not *and so is the kingdom of hell*, but rather *and so is the kingdom of quotidian ordinariness*.

A firm and frank recognition of the book's peculiar placement on the spectrum of literary propriety or decorum is indispensable to a fruitful reading of it, and such critical unfriendliness toward it as has gotten into print over more than a century can be traced to commentators' resistance to its being what it in fact is, to its working out of its own hypotheses according to its own direct, internal imperatives rather than theirs. *Culture and Anarchy* is a modern expression of a perennial outlook, both ancient and modern, Christian and secular: it is an enlargemnt into political and social relevance, that is, into the daily life of man in his public actions and relationships, of the "style," that is, the manner and meaning, of classical, Christian, and post-Renaissance humanism. Its dependence on the dialogues of Plato, especially the *Charmides* and the *Protagoras*, is obvious, as is its use of the Aristotelian technique of conceptual winnowing; but obvious, too, is that Arnold has subjected his models to such a thoroughgoing metamorphosis of application and literary manner that his book is *sui generis* even in the tradition of humanistic apologetics. His topical metaphors are aggressively contemporaneous. The historical construct by which he mythicizes the archetypal contention between doing and thinking in the cultural-spiritual history of the West is, though not absolutely unique, so distinctive and contextual that it is always identified with him in the English-speaking world. His creation of a narrative *persona*, a mark of the book's essential literariness, supplies the perfect strategy for keeping the humanistic perspective which he has chosen to represent wholly intact while visiting upon his narrator an ingratiatingly ironic fallibility that implicitly concedes how imperfect this pursuit of perfection can be without letting his weakness interfere with his faith.

The goal, the method, the range of the book are all seeded in the words of Montesquieu and Bishop Wilson at the beginning: "To render an intelligent being yet more intelligent" and "To make reason and the will of God prevail!" It is not the fanaticism of the proletarian revolutionary but the deceptive plausibility of the Liberal spokesmen for the middle class that constitutes the book's focus. It is they who are the power brokers and *soi-disant* philosophers, the parlimentarians and policy-makers, of the age—ardent, vocal, influential, and second-class. They constitute current "authority," busily making laws in the name of order without any adequate notion of the true seat of law or the real source and beauty of order. Hence, they are mirror-images of the age and, since they have said and done things publicly, they become splendid devices by which to show their constituents that "all manner of confusion" (anarchy) has arisen "out of the habits of unintelligent routine and one-sided growth" (191) which they reflect. It is not the worst of all possible worlds, but it certainly is not the best. It is the most ordinary of human situations, and it is susceptible of redemption through properly directed insight *("Know thyself")* and simple faith *(Believe in thy best self).*

Culture and Anarchy has none of the apocalyptic rhetoric of the nineteenth-century Romantic revolutionaries. Its rhetoric is freed from the cataclysmic urgency of Carlyle's crisis of survival in *Past and Present* by Arnold's faith in what the Duke of Wellington had described as "a revolution by due course of law" (135–36), which Arnold enlarged to encompass the "law" of human nature; by his subscription to Plato's unfettered, idealistic conception of "the desire which . . . 'for ever through all the universe tends towards that which is lovely' " (185); and by his intuition that there was at the moment a pervasive national "weariness with the old organisations" and so real, if "vague and obscure," a desire for "transformation" that "his is for the next twenty years the real influence who can address himself to this" (228). But Arnold intuited, just as surely, that his generation and the generation coming on had developed a resistant distrust of the furious stridency of critic-moralists like the later Carlyle and of the volatile Romanticism in which such "harsh, uncouth, difficult, abstract, professional, exclusive" investitures of knowledge appeared to take place (113). Such rhetorical intemperance made "a dreadful havoc in the heart" (133, Bishop Wilson), contradicting the gradualness with which "nature would have all profound changes brought about" (205). There was too much of the Jeremiah in such men, and Jeremiah was "just that very one of the Hebrew prophets whose style" he admired "the least" (88)—too little classical, too "incomplete and mutilated" (236).

A generation growing weary of its routine arrangements and distrustful of rhetorical firestorms was, despite its desire for transformation, not to be reached through the falsetto of lamentation or the melodrama of other forms of emotional inflation and extravagance. They had had more than enough of that sort of seedy Romanticism. It was their reason and their imagination that needed renewing, their capacity for aesthetic joy rather than their ordinary tolerance for flattery and high-minded overstatement—their "natural talent for the bathos" (147 and *passim*)—in re-enforcement of arguments that had begun to pall. It was a classic human situation for which there was a classical *literary* solution. The comedic formulations and practice of the Greeks, as masters of a rhetoric of corrective deflation and of subtle moral reconstruction, were perfectly suited to the nature and range of the problem as Arnold had conceived it: the very tropes with which he had characterized the situation ("confused, loud-talking, clap-trappy") shows that it had taken shape in his critical imagination around the metaphor of style—*style is the man/style is the nation.*

Arnold's adoption and transformation of a classical solution accounts for the recurrent sense of *déjà vu* that *Culture and Anarchy* generates. The book is reminiscent of that superb renewal of the classical moralist tradition undertaken by the generation of Pope and Swift and embodied in such masterpieces as Pope's *The Dunciad* and Swift's *The Battle of the Books.*[13] But Arnold effects a very different kind of literary metamorphosis—more genial, far less conspicuously rooted in analogies with the epic, only very occasionally allowing his wit to wield a hammer-blow. The texture of his apprehension is altered by the addition of the "sweet reasonableness" of Jesus to the *epieikeia* of Socrates, and his strategy of conversion is monitored by his efforts to give his readers personal experience of the truth of Socrates' "simple, spontaneous, and unsophisticated" assertion that " 'The best man is he who tries to perfect himself, and the happiest man is he who most feels that he *is* perfecting himself' " (167–68). This strategy makes Arnold's mythos very different from those of Pope and Swift.

The mythos or working fable of *Culture and Anarchy* is, like its dualism, delicate, tentative, and fluid. It was meant to be imaginatively co-operant with the "vague and obscure" desire for "transformation" whose presence Arnold intuited in the national psyche, and to have made his design upon a somewhat skittish audience too obvious and purposeful would have jeopardized its affectiveness. But as a design in the distance, it is a real and indispensable dimension of the book. Given that the subject is metamorphosis or "transformation," the action or "plot" is the resolution of the dramatic conflict between two metaphoric contenders or antagonists, *culture* and *anarchy*, in such a way as to avoid merely substituting one routine, unimaginative way of seeing one's life in this world for another routine, unimaginative way, that is, to avoid a mere exhange of complacencies. To achieve this elusive goal, the narrator must "do the thing shall breed the thought," must demonstrate in his own person that the end is implicit in the means, that, if undertaken in a genuine spirit of conscientiousness, the method of the book—"reading, observing, thinking" with a clarity uninhibited by special class or "club" interests or by such ordinary self-interests as physical comfort, material security, and routine notions of respectability—is the goal of the book.

In short, a truly enlightened and circumspect engagement with one's acts of living is the beginning of a process of imaginative self-redemption that can never lead to the perfection which is its goal, but which, even in its initial stages, is a verifiable source of the imaginative joy that provides the spiritual energy for further efforts in the same direction. It is this that justifies seeing the spokesman for culture in the text as a narrative *persona* rather than literally as Matthew Arnold. He becomes a complexly characterized contender in the book's central comedic antagonism, fallible but dependable on the whole, an actor as well as a listener, a functional literary metaphor. And Arnold's casting of himself in the role of himself-not-himself is instructive in an almost paradigmatic way: it exemplifies how dispassionate attentiveness metamorphosizes the ordinary self into a different life-role (as, implicitly, passionate inattentiveness does also) and, for the reader willing to experiment with the process that the book recommends, is a monitory preparation for the kind of *ad hominem* criticism that the assumption of this life-role is likely to provoke from those who have had little experience of it.

Indeed, Arnold's extension of his mythos outward to include his least friendly critics as well as inward to involve his sympathetic readers in a ritual of co-participation may be the subtlest index to the books's imaginative autonomy. He seems to have built into his overall strategy the necessity for the special kinds of critical dissatisfaction that *Culture and Anarchy* from the beginning provoked as a part of the technique, the "literary art," by which he assured the book's continued vitality. Few books in English so forthrightly topical have maintained such a persistent critical interest, have so successfully resisted the ever-present urge of succeeding generations to reduce its significance to an essentially historical one.

Though its contemporary trappings are far more plentiful than are those of *The Idea of a University*, for example, it has not slipped into a historical frame even to the degree that Newman's most analogous text has. This would seem to be the result of the book's mythic/metaphoric/fabulous center of imaginative dynamism, and the extension of the mythos outward is a dimension of that dynamism. Arnold's efforts to collect the usable criticisms against him while the book was appearing serially is an important part of the history of the book's evolution.[14] When one considers the close similarities between those original criticisms and succeeding ones, a persuasive conclusion is that the kinds of criticism to which the book has been subjected are actually a part of the book's own expectations, essential to its continued vigor. Alexander Macmillan had seen the point as early as July 25, 1867: "Your critics and opponents increase your influence for good."[15] Thus, in the spirit of the book's carefully calculated irony, Arnold's detractors are actually made to play a part in Arnold's sophisticated cultural drama.

The narrator's antagonists are such as to sustain the book's comedic integrity, its generic literary decorum, and they exactly fit his intention of gradually drawing the capable and sympathetic co-participatory reader into making more refined distinctions than has apparently been his wont. They are, for the most part, young, gifted, impressive, and off the mark—second-rate, not by natural endowment, but by habit of mind. They are more than reasonably complacent, more than reasonably sure that they have diagnosed the social problem and found the political solution, although less than reasonably informed about how people in other places and in other eras have sought to remedy analogous situations. They have not submitted their motives to such a reasonable degree of self-scrutiny as to recognize possible differences between their real and their declared rationales, and they tend to react to any contradiction of their position with somewhat more than reasonable fierceness.

In other words, his antagonists are humanly barometric, neither ominous villains nor authentic guides, but dependable measures of ordinary human nature plausibly maneuvering in a civilized social state not visibly under threat from external forces and not finely tuned enough to recognize the enemy within. They are our own unexamined political and social selves, and the narrator's gradual and generally effective erosion of their credibility through submersion in a medium of ironic skepticism and carefully scaled deflationary understatement that processively strips them of their patina of plausibility is his strategy for detaching us from our routine faith in our ordinary selves, while preparing us, without the precariousness of confrontation, for a role shift of which this ourselves-not-ourselves perceptual perspective is the elementary pattern.

Social radicalism is not his focus, but social torpor is. He fully recognizes that the proletariat is a quite distinctive force that will lay a very different hand upon the future. He sees this class, however, as an undefined, unpredictable force with whom middle-class spokesmen with nonconformist tendencies are playing highly fanciful theoretical or rhetorical parlor games, while remaining wilfully blind to the devastating truth that even the rudiments of urban anthropology would teach them. What he calls the "populace" in Chapter III is germane to his purposes for three specific reasons: because of the inevitable tendency of upwardly mobile members of their class to ape the class above them (Mrs. Gooch's Golden Rule, 122); because, in the metaphoric sense in which the term is used, we all have a portion of "populace" in our makeup and in our usual response to life; and because the inadequacy of the middle-class Liberals' apprehension or admission of the real situation of the populace and of its likely patterns of response is a stunning illustration of their social and political incompetence.

But the middle-classness of the middle class is Arnold's central subject, and his goal is not to shock or to comfort, but to awaken. Moreover, the fact that the central antagonism of the book is so precisely scaled rather enlarges than shrinks its significance. Middle-class Liberals are the manipulators of the reform spirit of the age. What they do is likely to affect the quality of life profoundly at the moment and to determine the character, the direction, the style of social and political metamorphosis for a very long time to come. Whatever shifts in external authority the future may bring, there will always be a middle class stereotyping its middle-classness. Hence an effort like that of *Culture and Anarchy*—to return habit, complacency, and spiritual hardness to solution, while at the same time guiding those who are weary of stolidity and desirous of transformation toward making their lives and the lives of others more humane and beautiful, more dispassionate and reasonable—will always have an import of large and complex proportions.

The protagonist of *Culture and Anarchy* is the reader. It is for his soul that the antagonists, who embody external manifestations of his inner dualism, contend. His ordinary self, more topical and contemporaneous in its definition than merely ordinary human nature's proneness to snuggle into a comfortable hole, has been nurtured on the philosophical theories, the moral and legislative dogmas, of men like Jeremy Bentham and Auguste Comte as glossed by such varied disciples as Thomas Buckle, John Bright, Frederic Harrison, Henry Sidgwick, Richard Congreve, and John Stuart Mill. Lord Macaulay, who was the stalking-horse of *Essays in Criticism*, is not even mentioned in *Culture and Anarchy*. His usefulness at a primary level had perhaps been exhausted. In any case, he had, since his death in 1859, rather drifted into the background. Even more important, however, Macaulay had projected a mammoth personality rather than standing for a philosophical school, and in *Culture and Anarchy*, Arnold diminishes the role of the charismatic individual in changing the course of human history, emphasizing instead "the natural current there is in human affairs" (110), while assigning alterations in culture to unconscious accretive tendencies among the many.

Bentham and Comte were the authors of two very different systems, of course, but the Arnold-*persona* sees them in the background of the present intellectual-spiritual difficulty, pairing them not only for their common dependence upon a rigid system but also for their fierceness in defending it: "some man, some Bentham or Comte, who has the real merit of having early and strongly felt and helped the new current, but who brings plenty of narrowness and mistakes of his own into his feeling and help of it, is credited with being the author of the whole current, the fit person to be entrusted with its regulation and to guide the human race" (109-10). Only two sentences from Bentham's *Deontology* were enough, he says, to deliver him "from the bondage of Bentham": " 'While Xenophon was writing his history and Euclid teaching geometry, Socrates and Plato were talking nonsense under pretence of teaching wisdom and morality. This morality of theirs consisted in words; this wisdom of theirs was the denial of matters known to every man's experience' " (111).

Culture abhors a Rabbi as nature abhors a vacuum, but

system-lovers adore a Rabbi, narrow and fierce, regarding true culture as "an impertinence and an offence" (111). In a long passage that appeared in the *Cornhill* but was cut from the book itself, a passage strongly reminiscent of Newman's style of combat in the pamphlets that were eventually modified into the text of the *Apologia,* Arnold drives home with relentless vigor and irony-run-to-sarcasm the justness of his view that the English disciples of Comte were "full of furious indignation with the past," while Comte himself, by the evidence of the "authorized version" of "the book of the master," was guilty of the "charge of system-mongering and machinery-mongering on an excessive scale" (504–06). Arnold probably cancelled this passage because he found that, in the stress of controversy, he had been drawn into the use of too fierce a rhetoric, thus risking a serious misdirection of the reader's attentiveness and compromising his speaker's emphasis on dispassion since *style* is clearly the chief instrument of psychological and spiritual measure and influence in *Culture and Anarchy.*

Throughout, the quotations from the "enemies" of culture are both fairly representative of their substantive positions and reflective of the peculiar state of their psychological growth, spiritual development, and temper. A reader-protagonist considering attentively and dispassionately the two sentences from Bentham quoted above, for example, will discover, after the initial stock response to their impressiveness has worn off, that they project a spiritual state that is neither attentive nor dispassionate, but peremptory and haughty. It is a stereotyped, formulaic style very much like that of a spokesman for the Government in the House of Commons rebuffing an objection from a member of the Opposition, a style of quick kill and very little circumspection. In this particular context, it invokes the ghost of the now silent, distant enemy of the friends of true culture, Lord Macaulay, with his sweeping dismissal of the ideals of the Greek moralists and his identifying *logo,* "as every schoolboy knows." In addition, a feeling of absurdity that explodes all possibility of serious reflection is provoked by Comte's " 'System of Sociolatry, embracing in a series of eighty-one annual Festivals the Worship of Humanity under all its aspects,' " his " 'Synthetical Festivial of the Great Being [Humanity],' " his " 'Metropolis of the Regenerated West [Paris],' " his " 'systematization of ideas conducting to the systematization of sentiments,' " and his "dating a preface the 15th of Dante, . . . an appendix the 22nd of Moses, a circular the 27th of Aristotle" (505–06).

When the reader-protagonist looks the other way, he sees Socrates and Christ in the place of Bentham and Comte, and instead of the fierceness and systematic rigidity of men like Buckle, Bright, Harrison, and Congreve, the ingratiating luminosity of such men as Montesquieu, Bishop Wilson, Goethe, and Newman, of men like Abelard, Lessing, and Herder. Nor does it need explicit pointing for a reader in whose inner ear still echo the words of Saint Augustine:

> "Let us not leave thee alone to make in the secret of thy knowledge, as thou didst before the creation of the firmament, the division of light from darkness; let the children of thy spirit, placed in their firmament, make their light shine upon the earth, mark the division of night and day, and announce the revolution of the times; for the old order is passed, and the new arises; the night is spent, the day is come forth; and thou shalt crown the year with thy blessing, when thou shalt send forth labourers into thy harvest sown by other hands than theirs; when thou shalt send forth new labourers to new seed-times, whereof the harvest shall not be yet." (113–14)

These are words that seem to speak directly to the inner self of the contemporary reader and to translate the very personality of Jesus into the "Canticles" of St. Francis of Assisi and "The Second Spring" of Newman. It takes no external help for such a reader to realize, when he sees *these sentiments* in *this style* characterized two pages later as "handing out [one's] pouncet-box" (116), that, indeed, "Intemperance in talk makes a dreadful havoc in the heart" (133).

Thus style, being the chief instrument of psychological and spiritual influence on the reader-protagonist of *Culture and Anarchy*, is, for the critic, an indispensable dimension of its mythos. It is not surprising, then, that the book's essential poetry can perhaps best be seen in the textual overlay, also mythic in character, of three worlds of style.[16] Most conspicuous is the contemporary world, the world being recorded, criticized, and corrected. This is the "style of anarchy," which is woven of the "facts" and "events" that give the book its modern rootedness and truth, its dense cluster of images by which we are induced to acknowledge the incontrovertibility of its portraiture. That is the way of the world of the 1860s without much serious doubt *as erected on the substructure of its own premises*. Arnold's way is a real way of seeing the epoch. By comparison, other ways of seeing it (e.g., those of Carlyle, Marx, Bentham's followers) seem duplicitous, thesis-ridden, and over-selective.

But the fact is that its metaphors are so precisely and so quantitatively cogent that it is also the contemporary world of the 1980s: nothing has changed but the images, and even they are alterations in the wording rather than of the objects designated by the wording (e.g., coal > oil > energy). If this is true, then it is also probable that an 1860s that can be altered to a 1980s can be in turn altered to a 1660s or a 420s B. C. Now we are talking about a timeless contemporaneousness rather than a provincial one, and the truth lies, not in literal topicality, but in poetic topicality. If, in any time frame, we select the authentic images well, we have thereby gotten in touch with timelessness by virtue of *seeing what in fact is*, not just because it is timely, but just because it is independent of time. For this, whether one is writing prose or verse—a *Divina Commedia* or a *Culture and Anarchy*, a *History of the Peloponnesian War* or an *Iliad*—one must be a literary artist (composer, poet, architect in language).

The second world, created like the first, is the world of words that is released by a serious effort to have these "facts" or "events" rationalized by two or more metaphoric voices or personalities. This is the archetypal contention, and its literary excitement lies in its action, architecture, and language. The "facts" are not the focus of interest, but the face one puts on the facts. The first world is obviously a language-world too, but it is language at a Baconian level, so to speak: the representation of data in language, a "table of discovery" that embodies, in a form of verbal translation, data of a non-verbal character. At least this is the illusion that enables us to make sense of it at the most primitive level. It may be, like time and space, a mere stubborn illusion, but it is very stubborn indeed. It is a second, more advanced order of "style," the general field in which we conceive of the notion of style. In *Culture and Anarchy*, for example, it is the "style" of the Liberal voices of the book (e.g., Mr. Bright, Mr. Harrison) in counterpoint with the "style" of the narrative voice (what is customarily referred to as "Arnold"): what they say is perpetually counterbalanced by what he says. That is the dialogue/debate/contention of the book, its conventional literary center. Not every book has this dramatic center. It is, however, a defining mark of *Culture and Anarchy* as well as of Plato's dialogues; that is how their literary machinery works. The facts have been superseded by perception in all of its complex reality: personality, implicit value-systems, recurrence to authority, response to challenge, concession, distinction, *ad hominem* attack, broad-based exposure, face-saving surrender. Of the three worlds being considered, this is the most quintessentially literary, the conversion of fact to an imaginative sense of fact, a highly formalized re-enactment of the age-old drama of human nature struggling to fulfil the best law of its own being.

The third world is that of *utopia*, the perfect world of which the authorial mind can realistically conceive—not a *Paradiso*, but one in which an ideally realized humanness can be presented, a harmonious state in which perfection can finally have, not mechanical achievement, but the consciousness of a faith verified by undiverted, visible, empirical evidence of emergence. It is a state beyond strategy, a mythic state imaginatively confirmed. It is like the first world in that it is not to be debated, but established, a "fact" or "event" or "truth." This third world is made possible by the existence of the first world, being a transubstantiation of its factual images. In a poem like the *Divina Commedia* or *Paradise Lost*, this is language's explicit goal: to create credible intimations of such a state in full-bodied, question-answering terms. In a book like *Culture and Anarchy*, it is an implicit goal, conditioning the drama of the second world and suggested or evoked by the way in which language perpetually threatens to shape itself into a coherent utopianism while in fact not doing so. It is the compromise with imaginative fulfilment of a wholly autonomous kind that critical prose must make in order not to *be* a poem.

Each of the chapters of *Culture and Anarchy* makes a distinct contribution to the suffusive impact that the book was meticulously designed to have, enlarging at a different center the consciousness of confusion which a stereotyped, inadequately informed, and exclusive state of mind leads to. It works within the parameters of a highly civilized social and political state like that which John Stuart Mill made the premise of his doctrine of individualism in *On Liberty*. But it shows that even the mechanisms of reform which Mill delineates are frustrated by the state of mind from which they emanate and upon which they depend for strategic guidance in problem-solving.

"Sweetness and Light" is strategic in an extraordinarily accomplished way. Arnold had appraised the enemies of culture very precisely. He knew that, if taunted, they would presume to make quick work of this effete purveyor of familiar, foreign, long-discredited cant about beauty and truth. He knew that they would read too superficially, think too perfunctorily, respond with too stereotyped a fierceness in too hard and glittering a manner to see the traps that he had carefully laid for them and that, as Thomas Henry Huxley had said of "Soapy Sam" Wilberforce, God would thus deliver them into his hands. In the self-blinding glamour of a heady, aggressive secularism coupled with the contempt for antiquity that they had learned from Bentham and Macaulay, they would miss the profound significance of this incipient blending of Hellenism with Hebraism, this alliance of Socrates and Jesus, and their ingrained irreverence would propel them into offending a crucial dimension of the very persons to whom they hoped to appeal. This, in turn, would provide Arnold with the route of access into the inner selves of these same individuals—their weariness with the present and their desire for transformation—that, despite current confusion, was a reflection of human nature's admiration for great and gentle people, its inherent longing for personal improvement, and its peculiar susceptibility to the influence of language.

The chapter begins in a very emblematic way, with the redemption of a word (*"curiosity"*), and invokes the service of a very archetypal principle: "we must find some motive for culture in the terms of which may lie a real ambiguity" (90). This "real ambiguity" is not, as first appears, in the negative sense in which the English use the term *curiosity* as opposed to the favorable sense in which the French use it, but in the Janus-like face of its most favorable import, both "scientific" and "moral." Thus Newman's "know" *(The Idea of a University)* and Carlyle's "do" (*Past and Present)* are reconciled in a view of human nature wherein the passion for knowledge and the passion for action are both defining characteristics; where the profound ambiguity (the archetypal contention) derives from man's imperfection, from his perpetual inability to be sure that he is in possession of the right reasons to do the right thing, or that even if his passion for knowing is well balanced and regulated, it is properly coordinated with his passion for doing. Moreover, the perfectionist passion which drives him despite the impossibility of its fulfilment constantly reminds him of his failures, wearies him with a sense of inadequacy, and tempts him to account the ordinary the best. Culture cannot alter man's archetypal nature, of course, but it can guide that nature, by that nature's own laws, toward fulfilment. Through the joy that comes of culture's progress in humanization, it can ease the distress of unfulfilled perfectionism. Culture is "the study and pursuit of perfection" (93), "Not a having and a resting, but a growing and a becoming" (94), and hence it does not require the sacrifice of the present joy to the future dream (104–05). It is especially timely at the present moment (92), but it is equally timely whenever its full authentic character opens up to the human consciousness.

Thus far the Arnold-*persona* has rooted his idea of the nature and function of culture in what can only be called a philosophy of man, and his reiterated ironic strategy of confessing his inadequacy in the awesome rigors of systematic philosophy, which was really his way of indicting the pretensions of his adversaries, should not blind one to his keen sense of the philosophical temper of the times and his brilliance in stripping philosophy of all that was "harsh, uncouth, difficult, abstract, professional, exclusive" in its ordinary style (113). He then moves to the analogy that is the most telling and encompassing in the whole book: the analogy between culture and religion. What he accomplishes in his handling of this analogy is strategically monumental. He establishes a real truth with a real distinction. Religion has been the "voice of the deepest human experience." Though its goals are identical with those of culture, however, religion has been narrower than culture in the pursuit of those goals, has not so fully promoted "a harmonious expansion of *all* the powers which make the beauty and worth of human nature . . . " (93–94). He removes from culture the onus of paganism or secularism, while implying that the sons of the philosophical radicals with whom he is contending are disqualified as judges of the true nature and character of culture by virtue of their alienation from or hostility toward religion. He prepares the way for a critical indictment of the ferocity of such mechanized and politicized religions among the Protestant Dissenters as are represented by an organ like the *Nonconformist*, inviting all those who are as put off by a "harsh, uncouth" religion as by a "harsh, uncouth" philosophy—those left stranded by the collapse of the Oxford Movement under the fierce attacks of middle-class Liberalism, for example—to find personal refuge in the humanizing process of culture. The religious analogy implicit in the merger of Hellenism with Hebraism is crucial to the argument of the book for several patent reasons: religion is the chief source of the kind of language Arnold is using and supplies the model of inner discipline with which his audience is most familiar; religion is likely to be the place where, in his audience's experience, the good as the enemy of the best is most visible and is often the most telling illustration of well-intentioned misguidance; and religion, the discipline most plentifully supplied with the mechanisms of redaction, is a rich treasury of that self-criticism which is indispensable to the central concerns of *Culture and Anarchy*.

The other chief analogy which the Arnold-*persona* uses is that of poetry—"culture is of like spirit with poetry, follows one law with poetry" (99)—and though, for reasons of scale, he touches the matter only briefly, it is important to recognize exactly what he does say. He creates a three-way analogy among poetry, religion, and culture that gives a futuristic turn to a metaphoric construct that, in "Hebraism and Hellenism," will be put to essentially retrospective or historical uses. Historically, religion has been far more important than poetry because of its broad, elementary emphasis on the moral rectitude of behavior. In the future, however, when poetry will absorb into itself, will be transformed by, "the religious idea of a devout energy," then will it have the power to "transform and govern" religion.

He sees as inevitable a tendency of poetry and religion to become one, as in fact they were one in "the best art and poetry of the Greeks" (101). When they become one again, the "devout energy" of Hebraism will have been added to the Hellenic "idea of beauty, harmony, and complete human perfection." Thus poetry, having been transformed by religion, will in turn transform religion. The catalyst for this double transformation will be culture, which is the expression of the laws of human nature's innate desire to know, to act, and to convert or improve itself. Hidden in this equation is an implicit faith in some future epoch of humanistic grandeur that surpasses even the Golden Age of Greece. Jesus himself, enlarged as a metaphor of moral beauty with a genius for language, is Western man's supreme symbol of such a metamorphosis, and each man of true culture contributes to the ultimate realization of this ideal and beautiful image of the race.

The tendency of even friendly critics of Arnold to assume that, since he was not belligerently systematic, he was, therefore, philosophically soft is an exact misreading of the case. The fact is that Arnold was so comforatable, so at ease, with philosophical thought that he could go straight to the premise and the method without the least need for quantitative demonstration. Throughout his career he evinced an exact if relaxed familiarity with the chief formulators of modern philosophical thought. Aristotle was for him as familiar as a friend, and his Platonism, as *Culture and Anarchy* clearly shows, had passed beyond thought into dramatic and verbal gesture. He could distill a philosophical treatise masterfully, as witness his essay on Spinoza in *Essays in Criticism.* Of course, his classical background made him impatient with the formulaic professionalism which modern philosophers customarily imposed upon their thought, while his role as a practical critic demanded that he deconstruct philosophical formulae and follow their impact closer to the cultural mainstream. Moreover, again because of his classical background, Arnold's imagination had early taken a distinctly dramatic bent, and his best prose, like his best poetry, had a personative or dramatic character that erased the philosophical rigidities of mind speaking to mind, filtering thought through the complex intricacies of a multi-dimensional *persona* who felt, dreamed, gestured, strategized, played with language, who enticed as well as thought.

Having established the religious and poetic character of culture, that is, what a profoundly beautiful idea it really is, the speaker then proceeds to show what "a far-off echo of the soul's prophecy of it" are the drab mechanical lives we ordinarily live and the drab mechanical religions we ordinarily practice. These things shrink very quickly by the standards of culture that have been carefully developed, and we awaken very abruptly to the discomforting realization that we have been substituting the "grand language" for the grand thing. We have allowed our language to become pretentiously sophisticated and called ordinary comfort well-being and hideousness beauty because we have lost contact with a genuine ideal of beauty and with the standard of genuine well-being. We have allowed the Roebucks and the Lowes to "debauch" our minds with a conventional "style of laudation" (108) and the Nonconformists to make us fiercely argumentative rather than truly religious.

"Sweetness and Light" is so imaginatively evasive because it is so tactical: it simultaneously causes the enemies of culture to disintegrate without a confrontal attack and builds its complex constructive apprehensions without conventional definitions and professional formulae. At the beginning of Chapter II, the narrator says that he has thus far "been insisting chiefly on beauty" (115). This assertion comes as something of a surprise, since the trope itself has not had a conspicuous presence in the chapter, until we remind ourselves of the kind of beauty to which it refers. It is the beauty seen by the inner eye, the mind's eye, or the soul's; it is the Platonic beauty of the *idea*, the philosophical idea, the moral and social idea, the *idea* of culture or of religion or of poetry. Arnold's notion of beauty encompasses the *itness* of things that we ordinarily talk about in such a vague and routine fashion that they never assume an individually distinctive character, a significant form, but exist forever in a mist of sentiment. But most of all the beauty of which Arnold speaks is the *idea* of man himself who, at his very best, forms such concepts and finds his true dignity and happiness in pursuing them. To have framed such an idea in the conventional manner of a modern philosopher would have deprived it of all distinction and have led to its being confused with the very idea of happiness that it was meant to replace. So Arnold employed the manner of the modern poet: he made his point dramatically, evocatively, accretively, metaphorically, and so successfully that many of those who have misconceived the manner have nonetheless felt its inherent force.

The perspicacity of Arnold in delaying the appearance of the "Anarchy and Authority" papers, which, with substantial revisions and a new preface, make up the balance of *Culture and Anarchy*, until he could "gather up all the murmurings [provoked by 'Culture and Its Enemies'] into one and see what they come to"[17] is well illustrated by the character of the next two chapters—"Doing as One Likes" and "Barbarians, Philistines, Populace." These "murmurings" went far beyond the well-known rejoinders by Henry Sidgwick ("The Prophet of Culture," *Macmillan's Magazine* [August 1867]) and Frederic Harrison ("Culture: a Dialogue," *Fortnightly Review* [November 1867]); the *Saturday Review*, the *Daily Telegraph*, the *Morning Star*, the *Daily News*, and, in America, the *Nation* got conspicuously into the act, along with many of the provincial newspapers.[18] There were no mortal hits, but the observations made by Arnold's critics were generally shrewder and more incisive than any that have been made since. Many of them had enjoyed a similar kind of intellectual training, and they were quick to recognize the chief outlines of his method of proceeding.

What they did not perceive, however, was the moralist mythos, the classical fable, into which "*Know thyself*" was being gradually converted. Both the tone and the substance of their rejoinders confirmed his judgment in several crucial respects: that his manner, which had caused an awful flurry in the henhouse of the periodical press, had been well chosen; that the *soi-disant* serious, practical, hard-working policy-makers of the world could, when sharply questioned, do little more than declare the virtues of being serious, practical, hard-working; that the *idea* of a thing, which can be acquired only through wide reading, attentive observing, and dispassionate thinking, activities with which ordinary human nature is either impatient or unfamiliar or woefully unpracticed, is everything—integrity, autonomy, and beauty making it the least vulnerable, hence the most truly practical, of all the objects of human endeavor and the conscientious pursuit of it the simple, wholly verifiable secret of self-humanization.

The idea at the center of "Doing as One Likes" is "the idea of *the State*" (122, 123–24, 134–36), and Plato, who taught us how to dream and to aspire toward our dreams' fulfulment, is reinforced by Aristotle, who taught us how to think. Thus, the argumentative method becomes rather more inductive, as "observing" is given first priority. The term *anarchy* begins to appear with increased frequency. To the intellectual confusion that had been its earlier import is added the ominous possibility of widespread civil disorder. The chapter fairly bristles with irony, some of it rather tough. This toughness seems literarily justified because these serious, practical, hard-working policy-men, who have interpreted a more urbane warning as "all moonshine" (115), must be more briskly shown that the only assurance the nation has that order can in fact be maintained is the Liberals' blind self-assurance, which the events themselves have discredited.

Four writers in the moralist tradition play a significant part in the chapter: two of them ancient (Plato and Aristotle), two of them modern (Carlyle and Mill). The ancient writers emphasize thought, the modern writers emphasize action. Plato, the philosopher of the human ideal, is a pervasive presence in the background, the guide to the idea-principle which is here being applied to the State. Aristotle is the explicitly declared model for the method of intellectual winnowing which, for all his ironic self-depreciation in philosophical matters, the Arnold-*persona* uses to perfection. He refers to it as "a plain man's expedient" and as part of the "lumber of phrases" learned at Oxford in "the bad old times" (126–27) and then proceeds to employ it with a rapier-like keenness and relentless inevitability against the enemies of the very humanistic tradition of which it is a symbolic expression.

Carlyle is subjected to a diminishment that requires of the reader who, like the narrator, remembers his "genius" in its glory days and feels a real debt of gratitude for his "refreshment and stimulus" a good deal of dispassion. But it is clear to any objective reader of the *Latter-Day Pamphlets* that Carlyle is a prisoner of an earlier age, the epoch of concentration following the Napoleonic upheavals, and that his endorsement of the aristocracy is an anachronism in a "modern" era marked by "the dissolving agencies of thought and change" (126). It is clear, too, that the feudalism inherent in Carlyle's metaphor of the Middle Ages in *Past and Present* has caught up with him. His myth has retained its rigidity while it has lost its charm. It is painful to see his relevance in tatters, but the critique is just and the technique circumspect. Though Mill's name is used only once in the book (111) and that not in this chapter, he is such a pervasive point of reference (as the very emphasis in "*the assertion of personal liberty*" [117] shows) that some commentators have read this chapter as a full-dress rebuttal of *On Liberty*.[19] But in light of the general vulgarization of the slogan "doing as one likes" which the narrator captures—its antipodal character as a voice played against Plato's voice, for example—it seems fairer to see the chapter as serving a subtler purpose. It suggests, rather, that this is what the philosophy embodied in *On Liberty* becomes when stripped of the gentle, delicate humanity of John Stuart Mill—fierce, raucous, and inhumane. The insight has larger ramifications: always look to the essential human idea rather than to the accidental practitioner because schools of thought that may look attractive in the hands of a founding genius very soon fall into the hands of third-rate persons who enjoy the impetus of the school without the genius that gave it an illusionary cogency.

There is also an ambiguity underlying the concept of "doing as one likes," but it is not the archetypal ambiguity contained in the term *curiosity*. It is absurd, as Arnold shows, though often romantically absurd. Behind this most modern of slogans as practiced by the aristocracy, there is the remnant pattern of the feudal baron visible in the lord-lieutenancy, the deputy-lieutenancy, and the *posse comitatus*, and this pattern expresses itself among the middle class in such offices as vestrymanship and guardianship. The working class, having no such feudal remnants and fast losing its feudal habits of subordination and deference, is expressing an anarchical tendency that shows what mechanical freedom without even mechanical patterns of restraint leads to (118–19). Still, despite the anarchical threat that results from the rejection of "the idea of *the State*" based closely on Burke and defined as an "organ of our collective best self, of our national right reason" (136), the modern Englishman either revels in the inspirational "force" of Mrs. Gooch's "symbolical" Truss Factory (121–22) or threatens to take up such a feudal alternative as "lead[ing] a sort of Robin Hood life under ground" (118). Moreover, such romantic absurdity has a darker, more threatening side. The zenophobia which is so self-laudatory when radiated outward toward the non-Englishman is positively internecine when radiated inward among the several classes of the nation, making them "separate, personal, at war" rather than "united, impersonal, at harmony," as "the idea of *the State*" would make them.

In "Doing as One Likes," the term *culture* is not insistently reiterated. Like Plato, it is a pervasive presence rather than an instrument of verbal bombardment. It is the source of "the idea of *the State*," and it is the process of transformation from the ordinary to the best self that makes such an idea both authentic and indispensable. But, with two notable exceptions, the technique of the chapter is one of exposure of both the vulgarity and the absurdity of the favorite national slogan when flooded with the light of reason and put into perspective by the need for national unity. One of the two exceptions to this overall technique is the abrupt shift in tenor which takes place after the quotation from Bishop Wilson on page 135, lines 24–25: we begin to talk, not about others, but about ourselves, and the process of meditative self-examination is renewed. The other exception is the transformation to which the slogan itself is put; "doing as one likes" attempts to make a social and political virtue out of fear of tyranny, whereas true virtue is rooted in faith, not fear. On the constructive side, therefore, "doing as one likes" can mean only doing what is best for ourselves collectively, the fulfilment of the very finest of our dreams.

To one who has observed the present situation, has read the best that has been known, and has thought the matter through, the issue takes on the metaphoric character of a choice between the social contract of Hobbes and the "idea of *the State*" of Plato, a choice between self-defensive fear and self-creative faith. Neither is realizable in theoretical perfection, so the question becomes which is the more integrated, autonomous, beautiful idea the pursuit of which will most fully enable us to discover and develop our best selves in order to bring us the happiness, not of material self-interest, but of the man "who most feels that he *is* perfecting himself" (from Plato, 168).

The rhetorical tradition in which the Arnold-*persona* works is that of simple plain-speaking in which both Socrates and Jesus had worked, free of the uncouth jargon, abstract principles, and structuralist formulae of professional philosophers and keeping as its focus the basic, clear, verifiable experience of a man resolved to examine the truth of his social and political—that is, his moral—character in the light of prevailing public arrangements. To the "sweetness" of Plato he adds the "light" of Aristotle, particularly the Aristotle of the *Nicomachean Ethics*. It is his Aristotelianism that draws "Doing as One Likes" and "Barbarians, Philistines, Populace" together, perhaps even determining the metaphors into which their subject-matter is converted. The still pervasive irony of "Barbarians, Philistines, Populace" becomes a bit more jovial in that it is more transparent and outlandish, becoming a more explicit clue to the book's character as a moral fable.

There is nothing particularly troublesome about the manifest intent of the new metaphors created to characterize the three principal social classes in "Barbarians, Philistines, Populace"; their explicit analytical meaning is cumulative and self-elucidating. But the spiritual ambience which the Arnold-*persona* creates around them is significant. He speaks of the need for "a shade more *soul*" (142), aligns himself more specifically with the moralists (e.g., 159), and recurs more frequently to the principle of "self-examination" (e.g., 151). Moreover, he quietly develops a complex network of implicit analogies between the conditions and workings of literature and the conditions and workings of the moral intelligence. In "Sweetness and Light," he had asserted that "If it were not for the purging effect wrought upon our minds by culture, the whole world, the future as well as the present, would inevitably belong to the Philistines" (97), and this assertion is an application to culture of the classical concept of catharsis as the chief moral function of poetry, especially of tragedy. In "Barbarians, Philistines, Populace," he not only draws an explicit analogy between culture and literature in the matter of "a scale of value for judgments" (148), he also employs literary concepts as an implicit way of enriching our idea of culture and of encouraging us "to look through the insistent . . . substance at the thing signified"[20]: empathy (143), "*talent*" or "a special and striking faculty of execution" (145), the power of the moment over the power of the man (146), the crucial difference between bathos and sublimity (147), the psychological effects of one's style upon oneself (155), the general function of style as an index to the quality of thought.[21] In fact, he provides a model for this sort of conversion in his reading of the style and substance of the *Times* as "a peculiarly British form of Atheism" and the style and doctrine of the *Daily News* as "a peculiarly British form of Quietism" (156–60).

It is within this spiritual ambience that the explicit clue to the book's character as a moral fable is given. The speaker asks us to bear in mind two things in considering "this new . . . and convenient division of English society" (143).

> The first is that, since, under all class divisions, there is a common base of human nature, therefore, in every one of us, whether we be properly Barbarians, Philistines, or Populace, there exist, sometimes only in germ and potentially, sometimes more or less developed, the same tendencies and passions which have made our fellow-citizens of other classes what they are. This consideration is very important, because it has great influence in begetting that spirit of indulgence which is a necessary part of sweetness, and which, indeed, when our culture is complete, is, as I have said, inexhaustible. Thus, an English Barbarian who examines himself will, in general, find himself to be not so entirely a Barbarian but that he has in him, also, something of the Philistine, and even something of the Populace as well. And the same with the Englishmen of the two other classes. (143–44)

This is an unequivocal clue to what the substance of *Culture and Anarchy* signifies. "*Know thyself!*" is clearly the center of imaginative interest and the real point of all the book's social and political machinery. More than that, it provides a structure through which the discipline of self-examination can be pursued and, in the analogy with literary empathy or detached, critical sympathy, it points to an image of ourselves-as-not-ourselves that takes complacency out of judgment and sentimentality out of indulgence. "They" are "we" at the distance of form and insight.

This does not mean that the social and political dimension, the revelatory machinery, is either unreal or unimportant. Indeed, in this imaginative context it becomes even more real and more important because if the metaphor collapses, the ultimate meaning becomes confused and trivialized. The social and political dimension works like "the poetry of nature" itself: things must really be what they appear to be in order for one to make the leap through substance to significance. The significance of "significant form" cannot be properly perceived unless the form itself is trustworthy. On the other hand, if one concedes that the intent of the creator of the form has or may have relevance to the way in which we see the form (observe it, think about it), especially if it is a written form, then the tests that we apply, the demands we make upon the character of the form (e.g., its scientific exactness or purity), are inevitably affected. We would hardly be justified, for example, in applying the tests of the literal-minded social scientist or statistician who endorses or condemns the results simply on statistical grounds since that would be to ignore the metaphorical dimension of the form and to require of it what, by its very nature, form cannot be. But we would be justified in applying the tests of literary criticism, both scientific and imaginative, and demanding that the form be true to the point at which literalness necessarily self-destructs and something different from literalness takes over.[22]

The second thing that we are asked to bear in mind is in some ways even more critically dramatic. Having refined the idea of class further, pointing out that each class ("they" still meaning "we") has an ordinary self with both "severer" and "lighter" sides that express themselves in quite distinctive ways, the speaker says: "But in each class there are born a certain number of natures with a curiosity about their best self, with a bent for seeing things as they are, for disentangling themselves from machinery, for simply concerning themselves with reason and the will of God, and doing their best to make these prevail—for pursuit, in a word, of perfection" (145). He then goes on to say that the function or effect of these "*aliens*" is to "enfilade" their class and to "hinder the unchecked predominance" of the "class-life." They generally have "a rough time of it"; and though their number is "sown more abundantly than one might think," the number "of those who will succeed" will be proportionate "both to the force of the original instinct within them, and to the hindrance or encouragement which it meets with from without" (146). Holding steady in our recognition that "they" are "we," we know that these "*aliens*" are aspects of ourselves, that this classless, humane instinct will vary in force from person to person, that we all have some degree of it, and that our capacity to realize its renovating power will depend to some degree on the character of our "moment" in cultural time. This "instinct" is the "possible Socrates" that "every man" carries about "in his own breast" (228). It is the "us" to whom the whole Socratic process is directed and that makes the reader the protagonist of *Culture and Anarchy*. It is the "*talent*" both of the New Testament parable and of the Greek myth; it is the poet that every man partakes of to some degree, the source of both his dignity and his joy; and it is the humanist's assurance that, even if he fails of ultimate fulfilment, he will not fail wholly.

The narrative *persona* of *Culture and Anarchy* ends the chapter "Hebraism and Hellenism" with one of the most circumspect, thought-provoking, and methodologically implicative sentences in the whole book. He has been speaking of the confusion of the current cultural situation brought about in England by the rise of Puritanism in the seventeenth century in contravention of "the natural order"—a Hebraic fundamentalism set against the strong new flow of Hellenism generated by the "Renascence"—and the consequent strong desire on the part of people of good sense for "a clue to some sound order and authority." "This we can only get," he says, "by going back upon the actual instincts and forces which rule our life, seeing them as they really are, connecting them with other instincts and forces, and enlarging our whole view and rule of life" (175). This masterful creative *reprise* gives renewed perspective to the book's assumptions, modes of proceeding, self-criticisms, and discoveries: the rootedness in human nature; the sensitivity to the tremendous power of social pressures and conventions over our individual lives; the dependence on philosophical or scientific truth combined with a deep distrust of the rigid, systematic over-simplifications of much elaborate, abstruse philosophy; the recognition of the indispensable need for imaginative historical perspective; and the resistance to persistent monistic tendencies to make a *contribution* to human development the *law* of human development. The sentence looks backward and forward to the line and operation of the whole book, of course, but it is a quite distinct and crucial convergence of language and concept, there being nothing quite like it elsewhere in *Culture and Anarchy*.

Rhetorically, this sentence connects "Hebraism and Hellenism" with "*Porro Unum Est Necessarium*," offering us a basis for understanding Arnold's enthusiasm for the "chapters on Hellenism and Hebraism" and his conviction that they "are in the main . . . so true that they will form a kind of centre for English thought and speculation on the matters treated in them."[23] Those "matters" include, certainly, the recovery of the metaphors *Hebraism* and *Hellenism* from the rhetorical misuse of others, specifically of Frederick Robertson and Heinrich Heine (164). One can reasonably credit the surge of energy and excitement in the chapters themselves to Arnold's sense of having found a new and happy way of representing his thought. Moreover, he was right in thinking that he had thus provided a central reference point for "English thought and speculation." Though one recognizes their independent presence in Heine and in such English documents, besides the sermons of Robertson, as J. R. Seeley's *Ecce Homo* and George Eliot's novels, Arnold's particular formulation has dominated the large and continuing interest in them.

But it seems quite unlikely that Arnold's enthusiasm was singularly centered on those metaphors, and an earlier reference to Robertson in a letter to his mother points to a different issue in a quite relevant way: "the English do not really like being forced to widen their view, and to place history, politics, and other things in connexion with religion," he said, after having asserted that Dr. Arnold's "greatness consists in his bringing such a torrent of freshness into English religion by placing history and politics in connexion with it. . . ."[24] In that sense, Arnold was, in these chapters, doing very much what "the English do not really like." He undoubtedly took great pleasure in making an original contribution to the intellectual tradition in which his father's "greatness" was rooted, while at the same time redeeming these metaphors, *Hebraism* and *Hellenism*, and converting history into poetic myth—the "two points of influence [between which] moves our world" (163–64)—thus giving to "this idea a more general form still, in which it will have a yet larger range of application" (163). This enlarged perspective suggests that the "truth" of these chapters is as much methodological as substantive, that the "meaning" is inherent in the "manner," thereby focusing one's critical attention on the exemplary methodological model by which this enlargement is achieved.

"Hebraism and Hellenism" is a superbly well-articulated example of the rhetorical use of the archetypal myth. Having initiated the book in what he perceived as the archetypal contention between the desire to "know" and the desire to "do," he then sees that conflict realizing itself in the history of Western civilization. He then chooses the two races with the most classic literary embodiments of their life-apprehensions still having wide currency to give root-names to these contenders for the spirit of man. Like Romanticism and Classicism, they are ever-present in the culture under study; therefore, in a useful, non-literal way, Hebraism becomes a manifestation of the Romantic impulse, with Puritanism one example of Romanticism seen from its obverse side, while Hellenism becomes a manifestation of the classical impulse, with a rigid and exclusive form of Humanism, corresponding to Puritanism in religion, as its negative counterpart.

The role of the Arnold-*persona* in the chapter is to free these metaphors and the human history which they should vitalize from rigidity and exclusivity, providing the reader-protagonist with an imaginative model for perceiving man's essential nature negotiating its way through time. His purpose is "a rhetorical purpose" (164) set against the inadequate rhetorical purposes of other historian-moralists like Robertson, Heine, and ourselves. What he primarily illustrates is the "rhetorical use" (164) of a classical method, having analogues in both Plato and Aristotle, of developing an exemplary substantive insight (an archetypal contention in man's very nature) in a richly textured metaphoric way, as he makes all necessary distinctions (*distinguo*) and concessions (*concessio*), preserving the integrity of the insight for "a yet larger range of application" (163) without having recourse to tautological, question-begging definitions and the "inter-dependent, subordinate, and coherent principles"[25] of the so-called philosophical systematists.

Having clarified his thesis as to the archetypal character of the contention (¶'s 1 & 2) and revealed his "rhetorical purpose" (¶ 3), the Arnold-*persona* characterizes in a dense, accretive fashion the contrast between the Greek and the Hebrew notions of felicity (¶ 4). He obviates any confusion between Hebrews and Christians by showing that "Christianity changed nothing in the essential bent of Hebraism . . . " (¶ 5), thus underscoring his conversion of a racial designation into a moral metaphor.

After again emphasizing the archetypal character of Hellenism and Hebraism, he insists strongly on "the divergence of line, and of operation with which they proceed" (¶ 6). He emphasizes yet a third time the archetype at the center of his conception, then delineates the Hellenic ideal of "beauty and rationalness" and the Hebraic unease with this ideal in its consciousness of "something which thwarts and spoils all our efforts" in pursuit of such an ideal (¶ 7).

"This something is *sin*": from the beginning, sin has been "a positive, active entity"—a "hunchback seated on the shoulders," the incubus, the cruel captor—of Hebraism (¶ 8). Though Hellenism was not in any absolute sense unsound, it was not, at the moment of Christ's conversion of the *style* of Hebraism, adequate, and "Hebraism ruled the world," a world that sought self-conquest by being "*baptized into a death*" (¶ 9). For a time and especially in its "wholesomest and most necessary" moments, Christianity was so wide, effective, and beneficent a force that Hellenism "was foolishness compared with it" (¶ 10). But it is a gross though common error to make either Hebraism or Hellenism "the *law* of human development" when, in fact, "they are, each of them, *contributions* to human development" (¶ 11). For example, neither Hebraism (*vide* Corinthians XV) nor Hellenism (*vide* the *Phaedo*) has dealt adequately with the "great idea" of immortality and with other great ideas that rise in their "generality before the human spirit" (¶ 12).

After emphasizing for a fourth time the archetypal quality of his central images, a reiteration which suggests the prototypical character of his rhetorical method, the narrator discusses the Renascence in Europe as "an uprising and re-instatement" of Hellenism with the Reformation as its "subordinate and secondary side," while in England the Reformation was its primary manifestation. He says that the English Reformation "never consciously grasped and applied" the Hellenic idea of the European Renascence and that its "pretensions to an intellectual superiority [over Catholicism] are in general quite illusionary" (¶ 13). But the Renascence as a whole, despite its "splendid fruits," manifested Hellenism's old weakness on the moral side, and a reaction against it set in (¶ 14). This reaction was peculiarly strong among the English and their descendants in America, who, despite their identity with philological and ethnological Indo-Europeanism and its imaginative response to "the multiform aspects of the problem of life," have yet a strong affinity for the Semitic predilection for "assuredness, . . . tenacity, . . . and intensity" in matters of "practical life and moral conduct" (¶ 15). In consequence, Puritianism arose with considerable ferocity in the seventeenth century and created, in England, a movement that "contravened" the primary movement of post-Renaissance Europe, which was Hellenic. Hence, *the problem*: "Everywhere we see the beginnings of confusion, and we want a clue to some sound order and authority." Hence, too, *the solution*: "This we can only get by going back upon the actual instincts and forces which rule our life, seeing them as they really are, connecting them with other instincts and forces, and enlarging our whole view and rule of life" (¶ 16).

Despite the undeniable importance of the chapter's *substantive* content, its *format,* i.e., its *methodological* content, is even more important. Its metaphors are absorbed into a yet larger metaphor. The clue that we "can only get by going back upon the actual instincts and forces which rule our life" is not commensurate with Hebraism and Hellenism: they are illustrative rather than conclusive, valuable as an initiation into a process that is itself the goal. That process is a re-creation in a transformed fashion of the finest legacy left by Socrates—*his method,* which is itself a metaphor of openness of mind and flexibility of intelligence put to the most conscientious of moral purposes, self-knowledge. The Socratic method is a structure in which manner and meaning ideally reciprocate each other and enable us all to "do the thing shall breed the thought." And that is the *idea* of the Socratic method.

"Hebraism and Hellenism" shows how saturated by Plato *Culture and Anarchy* is. But it is not merely Plato modernized; it is Plato in a new and original context that erases the sterility of re-statement and gives Arnold the opportunity to co-create with Plato, to employ fully his literary-spiritual heritage while adding to it. Rooted in the scientific theories of the philologists and ethnologists, his dramatic historical-metaphorical fiction of man moving between Hebraic and Hellenic poles enables him to add Saint Paul to Plato, creating a fresh myth of Western man. Moreover, it provides him with the opportunity to add Aristotle to Plato (Chapters II and III added to Chapters I and IV) and to re-establish, in a world increasingly enamored of the Hegelian dialectical formula, the call upon our attention of a more fluid and culturally serviceable Socratic method. Finally, the "science of origins" which had arisen in France and was gaining increased attention among the new historians could, Arnold shows us, be fruitfully employed at a poetic distance that saved it from the methodological rigidity that tended to make it dangerously fanciful.

Architecturally, "*Porro Unum Est Necessarium*" completes the curve of *Culture and Anarchy*. It begins to gather together tropes from Chapter I, to echo more insistently its metaphors of machinery, and to work again variations on the theme of truth's relationship to beauty: "But many things are not seen in their true nature and as they really are, unless they are seen as beautiful" (184). The literary future to which it looks is not Chapter VI, which is a sort of casebook or table of political applications, but *Literature and Dogma*, the author's next classic critical text. Hebraism and Hellenism are still working metaphors, but they are knitted into the text's overall patterns of imagery and are subdued to the book's general, ongoing arguments. In the final paragraph, the Arnold-*persona* enacts an intimate sort of *vale* to the reader who has come the whole route:

> And now, therefore, when we [you and I] are accused of [a rehearsal of the chief charges] . . . , we shall not be so much confounded and embarrassed what to answer for ourselves. We shall boldly say that . . . the best way is . . . getting our friends and countrymen to seek culture, to let their consciousness play freely round their present operations and the stock notions on which they are founded, show what these are like, and how related to the intelligible law of things, and auxiliary to true human perfection. (191)

Or, in the sense of the Buddhist fable with which he had begun *On Translating Homer*, having been converted, convert.

The natural outgrowth of *Literature and Dogma* from this chapter seems, in retrospect, almost inevitable. Arnold took his text from the Vulgate version of St. Luke's Gospel 10:42—"But one thing is needful"—and he wrote to his publisher, "I think with great pleasure of the Nonconformists reading in this month's Cornhill my discussion of their favourite text with them."[26] What he is basically criticizing is the Puritan myth of the magic wand, that is, the use of the Bible as a mechanical talisman, and some of the critical points he makes will be developed fully in *Literature and Dogma,* which is an elaborate exercise in the redemption of language. He applied to St. Paul's Epistle to the Romans a principle that Pater would later dramatize in the opening paragraph to the "Conclusion" to *The Renaissance*: "all writings . . . , even the most precious writings and the most fruitful, must inevitably, from the very nature of things, be but contributions to human thought and human development, which extend wider than they do" (181).[27] He links the idea of resurrection—"*risen with Christ*"—with his earlier discussion of "*baptized into a death*" (170), showing that the Puritan conception of resurrection "after the physical death of the body" is "mechanical and remote" compared with the apostle's "living and near conception of a resurrection now," which is what St. Paul means in nine cases out of ten when he "thinks and speaks of resurrection" (183).

When Arnold in "*Porro Unum Est Necessarium*" applies the principle of literary exegesis to the language of the Bible, he finds that St. Paul, "in trying to follow with his analysis of such profound power and originality some of the most delicate, intricate, obscure, and contradictory workings and states of the human spirit," used language "in the connected and fluid way" in which literature always uses language (182). He says that *homo unius libri est homo nulli libri,* the man of one book is the man of no book: "No man, who knows nothing else, knows even his Bible" (184). Perhaps most fascinating of all, he implants the idea that Christ was a literary critic of the text of the Old Testament, renewing its original intuition. Christianity, he says, "transformed and renewed Hebraism by criticising a fixed rule, which had become mechanical, and had thus lost its vital motive power . . ." (187–88).

In their most generalized form, the metaphors of "*Porro Unum Est Necessarium*" express an anxiety over a visible tendency toward the monism that, in both its intellectual and its psychological manifestations, has been so defining a characteristic of the modern period as well as one of its most curious paradoxes: as the need for circumspection has become more urgent, the movement toward single-mindedness has become more pronounced, almost as though increased scientism had resulted in mental constriction. The narrative *persona* shows a sensitivity to the opposite danger, the moral paralysis resulting from an over-refinement of man's analytical powers that concerned such writers as Sienkiewicz *(Ohne Lehr)*, Goncharov *(Oblomov)*, and Conrad *(Victory)*: "The notion of this sort of equipollency in man's mode of activity may lead to moral relaxation; what we do not make our one thing needful, we may come to treat not enough as if it were needful, though it is indeed very needful and at the same time very hard" (185). But he considers his "Mr. Smith" as the more widely representative and fatal "type" and the "havoc" made in his life more largely cautionary. Mr. Smith's high-minded but grotesque Puritan "fetish," his fear of perdition, had provided entry for the less high-minded though equally grotesque fetish of making money, supplying the paradigm of its "violently morbid" development: "It is because the second-named [fear of perdition] of these two master-concerns presents to us the one thing needful in so fixed, narrow, and mechanical a way, that so ignoble a fellow master-concern to it as the first-named [making money] becomes possible; and, having been once admitted, takes the same rigid and absolute character as the other" (186–87). It looks backward to Carlyle's characterization of "the hell of the English" as not making money and forward to Tawney's *Protestantism and the Rise of Capitalism*. Most of all, however, it captures with horrifying vividness that stultifying literalness which, long after Biblical fundamentalism has drifted into the background, still possesses the fetish-fixated materialist mind.

The suggestion that "Our Liberal Practitioners" is external to the basic architectural unity of *Culture and Anarchy* does not mean that it is of minimal significance. On the contrary, it supplies a sort of *practicum* by which the narrator can show how his principles apply to the current social and political situation and by which the reader can appraise the genuine usefulness of the method. Three of the issues (the disestablishment of the Irish Chruch, the Real Estate Intestacy Bill, and the attempt to enable a man to marry his deceased wife's sister) are pretty much lost to the current reader in the history of the times, but this has two distinct advantages: it shows how transient were most of the concerns that provoked such political passion and induced their advocates to costume them in such deceptively unctuous language; and it allows us to be attentive and dispassionate toward both the issue and the method, having no interest in the outcome to conflict with our dispassion. The fourth issue, that of free trade, is very much alive still, and this permits us to judge another crucial quality of Arnold's approach—the adequacy with which he develops the issue within the limits of rhetorical propriety which he has imposed upon the book. His narrator expresses satisfaction on the question: "For often by Hellenising we seem to subvert stock Conservative notions and usages more effectually than they subvert them by Hebraising" (220). But the question remains: does Arnold, within the space of fewer than ten pages, give adequate perspective to the issue of free trade as compared, for example, with Ruskin's much more expansive treatment of it in *Unto This Last*?

The answer to the rather surprising question is that he does, and the reason is that which Arnold gives: the voice of this critique Hellenizes, while that of Ruskin Hebraizes. *How* to think is Arnold's subject; *what* to think is Ruskin's. The ineptness of the official world's measuring and massaging of the issue by escaping into reassurance and irrelevance is the focus of Arnold's attention, while Ruskin attacks the rank immorality that results from the institutionalization of the system and the tenuous philosophy upon which it is founded. It is not that Arnold is less sensitive than Ruskin on either issue. His stunning quotations from the *Times* (211, 213–14) and his pinpointing of the "two axioms" of "our free-trade friends" (211–12) are evidence enough that he saw both the intellectual blankness and the philosophical chaos of the situation. He also opens a sufficient window on the vivid reality of human degradation: "such a multitude of miserable, sunken, and ignorant human beings" (216); "children eaten up with disease, half-sized, half-fed, half-clothed, neglected by their parents, without health, without home, without hope" (217).

But it is Arnold's premise that how intensely *he feels* about the social course the world is following under the banner of free trade is not as crucial at the present time as *how clearly people in general*, especially people in policy-making roles and their constituents, *think* about it; it is, he holds, "right reason" rather than plague-struck passion that ultimately effects "the will of God." If one considers this altogether too Apollonian for a Dionysian world, he may yet recognize that it is the best and most helpful alternative in a world showing ever-stronger chaotic and violent tendencies ("anarchy"); that it embodies a steady faith in modern pluralistic man, the child of the Reformation–Renaissance who has lost his fundamentalism while clinging desperately and mechanically to his individualism; and that it is not Mill's sense of the diminishment of eccentricity but Arnold's sense of the emergence of chaotic fanaticism that more precisely identifies the greatest danger of our time.

In the brief "Conclusion" to *Culture and Anarchy*, the Arnold-*persona* shows how little capable he is of intellectual drabness or rhetorical perfunctoriness. At the end of a long, necessarily reiterative, and classically controlled *literary* demonstration from which popularly emotive appeals have been carefully excluded and into which a reader-protagonist has been drawn with utmost gradualness requiring great and precarious tact, because the process of redaction (culture) appears at first sight to be so grossly incommensurate with the dimensions of the problem (anarchy), the narrator yet holds steady, neither simply rehearsing what has already been said nor yielding to the enticement of peroration, thus rupturing the tone of clearheaded faith that has been carefully established and maintained. Instead, and by analogy with music, he reinvokes the dominant themes of the preceding movements, as he brings them to imaginative resolution in a way that is both familiar and new.

The identification between the Arnold-*persona* and the reader-protagonist is now assumed to be complete and operates fully as an assumption, "we" saturating the conclusion in a new and quite intimate way. The articulation of faith in ourselves makes possible the articulation of an intenser faith in the sacredness of the "idea of *the State*," our collective best selves, and, in an oblique analogy with the sacraments of religion, that sacred efficacy is placed above and seen as independent of the moral condition of those administering it. As in religion, too, faith enables the Ideal State to function in its imperfect, quite ordinary present condition just as the Ideal Church is enabled to function in a quite comparable condition (224). Such is the utopianism of our awakened best selves that there will always be a discrepancy between even our best realizations and our ideal conceptions.

So our real problem is not the discrepancy between the best and the ideal, but between the good and the best, and it is only after we have had some experience of the best that the relative closeness of even the good to anarchy will be perceptible. Moreover, the two states of mind denied to "*believers* in culture" (226, emphasis added) are the same as those denied to Christians in Christianity's most gracious and debonair period, that is, "despondency and violence," because they turn man in the direction from which redemption can never hope to come, self-destruction and the destruction of the order upon which even survival depends.

It is in this spiritualized ambience that the Arnold-*persona* separates himself, for the one and only time, from Aristotle. In the *Nichomachean Ethics*, Aristotle had stressed the idealism of the young and had seemed to despair of the conversion of the great "mass of mankind": " 'to *their* lives, who can give another and better rhythm?' " (225). Putting his faith in the spiritual contribution that "the long discipline of Hebraism" has made to Western man since Aristotle's day, the Arnold-*persona* refuses to "admit and rest in the desponding sentence of Aristotle" and "dare[s] to augur" better for modern man than Aristotle had augured for his Hellenic contemporaries.[28] Finally, the charge which the Arnold-*persona* delivers to the reader-protagonists, whose work now becomes that of "the sovereign educators," is an apostolic charge. In language suffused with the quiet energy of poetry rather than the inflation of self-conceit, he ends where he had begun, serenely orchestrating the spirit of both Jesus and Socrates: "Docile echoes of the eternal voice, pliant organs of the infinite will, such workers are going along with the essential movement of the world; and this is their strength, and their happy and divine fortune" (229).[29]

No Englishman of equal critical genius has ever shown himself more intellectually just than Matthew Arnold. It was not easy for a man of such genial, lively spirits as Arnold to spend one's lifetime taking the moral (the intellectual, the aesthetic, the behavioral) inventory of one's contemporaries, especially of that segment or class of one's contemporaries with which he most strongly identified. Yet, it was just that role that Arnold's sense of conscientious duty made him play. A gift of insight peculiarly his own made it incumbent upon him to lend out his gift, not because it was singularly and dogmatically true, but because it was distinctively cogent, and hence needed, in an expansive and confused age, to be considered. Those who find him complacent here, extravagant there, should consider that, in an ardent crusade pursued so outspokenly for thirty-five years, the surprising thing is not that there are grounds for critical dissatisfaction, but that those grounds are ultimately so few and so relative.

While his Socratic querying was relentless, he offered no systematic codification as an alternative to the one he was challenging. Therefore, he did not create a "school" of thought, a systematic philosophy with which a substantial number of persons could identify and which would, in turn, enjoy the quantitative weight of their numbers. Like Plato and Aristotle, who were the chief models of his ideal of human rationalness and of his intellectual method, his "system" could be organized only by the individual and only within himself. To be an "Arnoldian," then, means, not that one has adopted a set of substantive beliefs. Rather, it signifies that one has come to the general position that his great happiness is to be found in the creative activation of those resources of his purely human nature not dependent for their satisfaction on his animalilty and that he has recognized the existence of a significant number of sacred texts which, if one will simply gain access to them and learn the secret of their way of looking at life, will serve as profoundly affective guides to growth in these peculiarly satisfying, non-sensual dimensions of one's humanity. It is not the saint that Arnold would make, nor simply the "Gentleman" who is the "great but ordinary end" of Newman's university. It is, in Aristotle's terms, a person fulfilling the law of his being individually and contributing to society's fulfilment of the law of its collective being.

This is why *reading* is the keystone of Arnold's three-part process of self-humanization. Great books (a) look at life (b) in a quintessential way; hence, they enable us to reach out to life unimpeded by the barriers of local time and local space, as they offer us various exemplary ways of looking at it. The counterpart to reading is *observing*, seeing for ourselves the clusters of live-experience available to us in our own time and space. The two ways of *seeing* are then fused through the third element in the process—*thinking*—by which we develop our individual insights into the life we get to know through the modes of perceiving instracted from the books we read. Thus, Arnoldianism is no more nor less than a classical critical process rooted, not in a system of thought, but in a faith in the self-redemptive resources of man. The locus of one's critical dissatisfaction with such a process should be either *the process* or *the faith* as measured against a preferable ideal or in comparison with some other writer who has followed a similar line of endeavor to better general effect. This is what makes *Culture and Anarchy* such a crucial literary text, not just in Arnold studies, but in the whole critical enterprise: it provides, in exemplary form, the fullest direct, internal evidence of both the Arnoldian ideal and the Arnoldian process. What is even more edifying in a critical moralist, it shows us to what severe standards a work of criticism should aspire while subjecting itself to just such standards.

NOTES

1. That is, the two introductory paragraphs to "Culture and Its Enemies" which, when Arnold gave the divisions of the book the titles we now know, he separated off and named "Introduction." All references to *Culture and Anarchy* are to *The Complete Prose Works of Matthew Arnold,* ed. R. H. Super (Ann Arbor: University of Michigan Press, 1965), Volume V, and are given in parentheses in the text.
2. The pieces collected into *Friendship's Garland,* a sort of companion-volume to *Culture and Arnarchy,* had chiefly appeared there.
3. Arnold's *New Poems* appeared in 1867.
4. Fitzjames Stephen's unfriendly remarks about Thomas Arnold which had prompted her son to write "Rugby Chapel" were still fresh and painful to Mrs. Arnold.
5. *Letters of Matthew Arnold 1848–1888,* ed. G. W. E. Russell (New York: Macmillan, 1895), I, 367.
6. *Letters,* I, 390, emphasis added.
7. December 5, 1867, as quoted in Super, V, 414.
8. November 25, 1865, as quoted in Super, V, 414.
9. April 5, 1869, as quoted in Super, V, 415.
10. *Letters,* II, 13.
11. Arnold had himself used both the metaphor and the psychological-moral state in "Stanzas from the Grande Chartreuse."
12. For a different view leading to very different extrapolations, see Walter J. Whipple, "Matthew Arnold, Dialectician," *University of Toronto Quarterly,* XXXII (October 1962), 1–26.
13. J. Dover Wilson, in the introduction to his edition of *Culture and Anarchy* (Cambridge: Cambridge University Press, 1932), has elaborated the transfer by Swift to Arnold of Aesop's fable of the Spider and the Bee ("Sweetness and Light").
14. See William E. Buckler, *Matthew Arnold's Books: Toward a Publishing Diary* (Geneva and Paris: E. Droz, 1958), pp. [85]–92.
15. Buckler, p. 87.
16. It is perhaps unnecessary to remind those familiar with John Holloway's fine chapter on Arnold in *The Victorian Sage* (London: Macmillan, 1953) that, though this essay touches many of the same terms—e.g., persuasion, techniques of dismantling the enemies of culture, irony—our conceptualizations of the essential literariness of *Culture and Anarchy* are fundamentally different.
17. Buckler, p. 86.
18. Super (esp. pp. 408–17, 422–25) gives a substantial representation of these and points to the very detailed studies upon which he has drawn.
19. For example, Lionel Trilling, *Matthew Arnold* (New York: W. W. Norton, 1939), pp. 259–65.

20. One of the rare limitations of the Super edition can be seen in the way "style" is indexed. Only entries referring to discussions of style are given, the important contextual uses of the metaphor being ignored. Thus we are disappointed in our hope that the index will work as a kind of simplified concordance.
21. Thomas Hardy, Preface to *The Dynasts*.
22. Patrick J. McCarthy's *Matthew Arnold and the Three Classes* (New York: Columbia University Press, 1964) suffers from inadequate attention to this critical principle.
23. *Letters*, II, 13.
24. *Letters*, I, 362.
25. This is the phrase, used reiteratively with ironic intent, by which Frederic Harrison's indictment of "Culture and Its Enemies" is pommeled. See Super, pp. 423–24, for a précis of this part of Harrison's "Culture: a Dialogue."
26. Buckler, p. 89.
27. Pater's sentence is this: "That clear, perpetual outline of face and limb is but an image of ours, under which we group them—a design in a web, the actual threads of which pass out beyond it."
28. Arnold's hope of self-transcendence also has a more practical strain than Plato's, who "expressly denies to the man of practical virtue merely ['That partaking of the divine life'], of self-conquest with any other motive than that of perfect intellectual vision" (p.167). Arnold retains the ideal of "the *φιλομαθής*"—"the lover of pure knowledge"—but throughout *Culture and Anarchy*, he insists on its practical serviceability to the nation.
29. The "Preface," like "Our Liberal Practioners," is not organic with the architectural design of *Culture and Anarchy*. Arnold no doubt saw it as an opportunity to do some good and to strip away some of the misconceptions that had accreted around his positions as taken in the serialization of the book. There are many good things well said, but the chief new inputs are his call for a reprinting of Biship Wilson's *Maxims*, his putting of the matter of the United States' separation of Church and State and its educational system back into proper perspective, and his tentative suggestions, based on the situation of the reformed Church of England during the reign of the Tudors, for a re-union of the Nonconformists and the Church of England and the association, through the principle of establishment, of the chief churches of Ireland.

Index of Primary Names and Literary Texts